The best course!

We would like to thank ...

If not for Carol Salvin, our cookbook designer, the history and recipes of the Holm family would still be scattered about on scraps of paper. Similar to sewing a quilt, she pieced together our stories, photos, artwork, and recipes. She skillfully guided us, cognizant of what needed to be done in the many aspects of cookbook development. For ten years, Carol has been dedicated to our project and joined us for family events to really experience the Holm family and the Circle H Ranch. She was instrumental in moving us forward from a dream of preserving our family history and recipes to a tangible memento that can be shared with all.

Many thanks to Mary Evans for her pre-edit of the manuscript, Beth Berkelhammer for her meticulous perusal of the recipes and layouts, and Michele Wall for her final proofreading before we went to press.

This cookbook has been a family project involving three generations, mainly Ione Holm's two daughters, Tilli Calhoun and Patsy Neely, and granddaughters Susie Calhoun, Merry Carter, Wendy Howe, and Nancy Mueller. Ione's spirit lives on in this cookbook. Without her, the current and future generations would not have these wonderful memories and stories. The extended Holm family and friends are to be acknowledged for their donation of recipes, photos, and memories.

We would like to apologize to the family members and friends whose recipes may not have made it into the cookbook. Due to a computer hard-drive crash, our very busy lives, and household moves, there were some recipes that we were not able to include.

We must also recognize the recipe testers. Friends and family rose to the occasion to donate their time, kitchens, ingredients, pocket books, culinary skills, and taste buds to test the recipes. Hats off to the chefs!

Maureen Abaray	Faye Cater	Josey Foscalina	Cindy Lotsey	Shelly Phillips	Polly Struthers
Sue Ackerman	Lisa Cochrane	Becky Foster	Candace Machein	Carolyn Piazza	Teri Tith
Kelly Albrecht	Suzanne Cofer	Mario Garcia	Lou Ann McCune	Judy Prima	Carleen Trites
Tiffany Albrecht	Dolores Connors	Steve Goodman	Nancy McKenzie	Alison Raymond	Melinda Vargo
Linda Andrade	Amie and Chris Conrad	Kerry Griggs	Mary McNeill	Fran Rebello	Brenda Vieux
Bobbie Baird	Earleen Cox	Phyllis Hallam	Sue Mears	Jane Robles	Melanie Vieux
Ellen Bell	Rosemary Cunningham	Gary and Jeri Holm	Margot Meskin	Judith Sanderson	Raelene Vieux
Kim Bonde		Warren Howe	Kimberly Moore	Patty Shirley	Marv Viramontes
Kristin Boutte	Peter Davidow	Eric Johnson	Bob Mueller	Jackie Stefanski	Janet Von Toussaint
Melanie Butler	Sandi Devin	Joanne Kamp	Paula Mueller	Jamie South	
Pat Byrne	Jane Drummond-Mullarkey	Shelly Keith	Robert Mukhar	Lori South	
Ken Calhoun		Teri Lambert	Beverly Norleen	Terry Spraggins	
Laina Carter		Diane Long	Melody O'Shea	Lillian Steinle	

The HOLM Family
COOKBOOK

*Some eat to live,
we live to eat!*

ISBN 978-0-9816570-0-4

Circle H Cowgirl Press
1896 Keeler Street
Livermore, CA 94550
holmfamilycookbook.com

All photographs included are the property of various members of the Holm family.
Cover and text design by Carol Salvin
Original paintings on front cover by Tilli Calhoun

Printed in China

DISCLAIMER

Women have been creating recipes since they first began preparing the meals that kept their families nourished and healthy. The methods and techniques of their successes have always been shared and passed on to family and friends. This collection of recipes has been gleaned from many generations of meals prepared by our extended family and friends. It is meant to honor and preserve the efforts of those cooks who have helped define our family celebrations and mealtimes. Many of these recipes that have been passed from generation to generation have origins that are unknown to us. While every effort has been made to avoid using copyrighted materials, we cannot review every book, magazine, and publication printed over the last century to be assured we are not infringing upon another's legal rights. If we have done so, it was unintended, and we are sorry. The recipe for a delicious dish is passed on; our hope is that you will enjoy our family's collection, too.

These days, we often interpret a recipe somewhat loosely, depending on our taste and dietary preferences and those of our friends and family. Feel free to replace the cream in a recipe with nonfat milk or reduce the quantity of butter—health, family, good food, and merriment are all ingredients for long life with laughter.

*Jamie South
with Papa's beans*

Table of Contents

*Standing: Buford Toney,
Desmond Teeter, Lou Gardella,
Dave Holm, Dick Holm
Seated: Dorothy Teeter, Helen
Teeter Kennedy, Ione Teeter Holm*

*Left to right: Jim Holm Sr., Kath
Kilgo, Richie Holm, Frank Holm,
Wayne Calhoun, Merilyn "Tilli"
Holm Calhoun, Sue Kilgo Boies*

Ione Holm, circa 1907

Ida Holm, circa 1900

Ione with schoolmates
Jack Williams (left) and
Bill McGlinchey (right)

Ione with her twins
Tilli and Frank,
April 1930

Ida Holm and friend Katie

Dedication **To Our Grandmothers**

There are caring people who impact our lives, whose influence stays with us forever. This cookbook is a tribute to our grandmothers, **Ida Jessen Holm** (Grandma Holm) and **Ione Teeter Holm** (Granny Holm), who, by their example, their patient teaching, their love and their wisdom, helped us to become who we are today.

Our childhoods were spent at Fair View, the Holm Farm, which was established by Carl and Ida Holm and was located on the Livermore-Pleasanton Road (now Stanley Boulevard) in the Livermore-Amador Valley of California. Golden fields of grain grew from one end of the valley to the other and were patchworked with farmhouses and barns, vineyards, and small orchards of walnuts and almonds. Four generations of our family lived on the farm.

Grandma Holm's Kitchen circa the 1930s. Original drawing by Tilli Calhoun

First generation	Carl and Ida Holm
Second generation	Walter, Arthur "Art", Bertha, May, Leslie, Gladys, and Warner "Dick" Holm
Third generation	Leslie, Jr. and Robert Holm; Merilyn "Tilli", Frank, James "Jim," Richard "Richie," and Patricia "Patsy" Holm; Carl Stebbins
Fourth generation	Tommy and Bobby Holm, Wendy and Lori Neely; Peggy and James, Jr. Holm

Carl and Ida Holm were of Danish descent. It is said that most people eat to live, but the Danes live to eat, and that the Danes are a gregarious, hardworking, frugal people who love their well-kept farms and gardens. This was true of the Holm family. Dick Holm said, "I hope I die in my garden like my brothers Walter and Art"—and he did.

At Fair View, the kitchen, which always smelled of strong coffee, bustled with activity—the clink of dishes and clanks and rattles of pots and pans, particularly at times when other workers were helping with tilling, planting, or harvesting. It was common to prepare five meals per day: a hot breakfast, lunch, dinner, a morning break, and and afternoon break for coffee and pastry, bread, and cheese. Meat and potatoes were always served at dinner.

The large bright kitchen had windows along the east wall, as well as many ceiling-to-floor cupboards for the dishes, pots, and pans. A large table was in the middle surrounded by at least seven chairs. The door on the south side opened to a porch with a sink where the men stopped to wash up and remove their hats before eating. A Grant Wood painting of a farm kitchen reminds one of those days—the white foreheads over tanned brown faces.

Settlers sought a better life

By Muriel Jelsma
Special to The Tribune

LIVERMORE — For years, Dania Hall on Second Street here was the gathering place for the valley's large Danish population.

Families arrived in open wagons and packed the hall each Saturday night.

Later those nights, the children slept in makeshift beds in the hall's upstairs while their parents continued to socialize below.

There were great holiday festivities with events for every age group.

In those days, immigrants had such strong ethnic ties that it was common for young men to send back to Europe for brides, rather than marry outside their group.

Danish immigrants — often called "Square Heads" because some were carpenters who carried square-headed hammers — were among the early settlers of the Livermore-Amador Valley.

... and rich land at-
... to Cali-

The Danish Lodge picnic, circa 1908. Grandma (Ida) Holm in front standing row, third from left. Grandpa (Carl) Holm, in front standing row, sixth from left.

8

The Danes in the San Francisco Bay Area

A story passed down in the Holm family tells that one of Ida Holm's forefathers was a Danish sea captain who sailed into the Bay when there were only seven houses in what is now San Francisco, California.

It is known that Danish whaling ships anchored in the San Francisco Bay in search of water and provisions. The height of the California Gold Rush was from 1849–1853. Many sailors deserted their ships to join gold seekers (known as the 49ers) in the placers of the Sierras. The majority had little success. Many had noticed the abundance of natural resources in the Bay Area—redwood forests, millions of wild fowl, large herds of game animals, fish in the rivers and bays, salt, and rich land that could produce hay, grain, and vegetable crops. Markets were available in rapidly growing San Francisco, which was booming with tents and wooden houses.

A young Danish sailor, Cornelius Mohr, left his ship in 1852 to find work as a carpenter and farmhand on the ranches around Alvarado in the Bay Area. In 1853 he purchased 200 acres of the Soto Land Grant. Many of the young Danish immigrants found work through Mohr. He became recognized as the founder of "Little Copenhagen" and "Germantown," which is now San Lorenzo in Alameda County. Cornelius Mohr's properties grew to include 360 acres in Pleasanton where his son, Henry P. Mohr, raised large grain crops, pastured range cattle, and became a noted breeder of Clydesdale and Shire draft horses. Henry P. had five daughters: Eileen, Ernestine, Mildred, Cecile, and Edna. They were family friends of the Holm family. Cecile recalled enjoying a visit at 4:00 p.m. on a Sunday at the Holm house and being delighted by the spread of food, which included delicious cream puffs.

Many of the young Danish immigrants had experience as carpenters and ship builders. They carried hammers with square heads and became known as "squareheads."

The immigrants planted crops and prospered. Some harvested salt from the land edging the Bay. Landings were built and barges and schooners carried grain, vegetables, fruit, salt, and wild fowl to San Francisco. Some also carried passengers and baggage to San Francisco and other local ports such as Alvarado, Alviso, Redwood City, and Pigeon Point. Roberts Landing, north of the mouth of San Lorenzo Creek in San Leandro, became the great shipping point for the surrounding area and from the Livermore and San Ramon valleys. Alameda County was formed in 1853.

In the San Leandro area, the Denmark Hotel in Mount Eden became the headquarters for Danish dances, lodge meetings, religious services, and other community events. Many of the immigrants were from the duchy of Schleswig-Holstein. This area had been fought over by the rulers of bordering Germany and Denmark for decades. Many would leave when they reached the age when they could be drafted into the military. Some immigrants spoke the language of both countries.

Ida Jessen Holm **Family History**

Grandma Holm was born Ida Jessen in 1861 in San Lorenzo, California. Her parents, James and Anna Jessen, immigrated from Denmark. They bore three daughters in the new land: Anna, Dora, and Ida. The East Bay of the San Francisco area attracted many Danes because its rich soil

Ida Jessen Holm

offered an opportunity to establish vegetable, grain and dairy farms and fruit and nut orchards. The dream of a Danish immigrant was to become a "landsman," impossible in their homeland where the nobility owned title to most of the land. Through hard work and frugal living, they prospered in the Bay Area. Later, many moved along the Alameda and into the Livermore-Amador Valley. The area between San Lorenzo and Mount Eden was sometimes called "Germantown" and "Little Copenhagen."

The 1860s were difficult years, plagued with disasters and scoundrels who came from all over the world, attracted by the lure of gold. Mothers of young girls would push their daughters under the bed when the clatter of horse hooves warned of unexpected visitors who might be intent on robbing or killing the inhabitants. In 1861 terrible floods drowned thousands of cattle in California. The years 1862 through 1864 brought drought; crops were lost, and animals died from thirst and hunger. Ida remembered a bull, insane with thirst, breaking through their front door. During this time, the family, including the three girls, survived by collecting the bones of dead animals and selling them to button makers.

The Jessen family moved to the Livermore Valley, where they lived near the Arroyo Del Valle Creek in a sycamore grove. Many years later, the area became known as Camp Comfort (the local brothel) on what is now Vallecitos Road. Their home was a small wood-frame house in the pioneer style. James Jessen established a picnic grove and listed his occupation as farming. Hundreds of Danes throughout the Bay Area picnicked at the grove, which today is known as Sycamore Grove Park and is part of the Livermore Area Recreation and Park District.

Growing up, Ida learned the many crafts pioneer women needed to survive: cooking, preserving eggs and meats in crocks, baking, gardening, canning, dressing chickens and animals for eating, making soap, washing clothes in a tub, starching, and heating a "sad" iron on the stove for ironing. Learning these skills prepared her to run a household when she married.

The Danes would gather for dances, card parties, picnics, and weddings. They encouraged friends from Denmark to immigrate to this land of opportunity. Carl Holm came to the United States in 1873 to visit a friend. Traveling by train through the Livermore-Amador Valley, he thought it would be a wonderful place to live and farm, and he hoped to settle there. He met Ida Jessen, who recalled, "He was a daring young man. He pulled me behind the kitchen door and kissed me."

Ida Holm with Tilli Holm

Carl and Ida were married at the Jessen home in the syca-more grove on July 11, 1880. The day after their wed-ding, Ida began cooking for boarders. Their first home was in the Tassajara area, northwest of Livermore. Ida and Carl were to have nine children, not uncommon in those years. Their first child, Walter, was born in 1881; Louis was born in 1883 and died in 1884; Arthur was born in 1886, Mabel in 1889, and Bertha in 1891. Chester was born in 1893 and died in 1896; Leslie was born in 1895, Gladys in 1899, and Warner (Dick) in 1900. There were no doctors, so a friend helped deliver Ida's children, and Ida helped deliver her friend's babies.

Carl and Ida recalled that hundreds attended their fifty-fifth wedding anniversary. Danes from throughout the Bay Area gathered to celebrate with the Holms.

Mona Detjens Holm and Ida Jessen Holm standing to the east of Fair View, near the hay field and Walter Holm's farm

Remembering

When I was a little girl, our family lived on the Holm farm in the big house with my grandparents Carl and Ida Holm. I spent so much time with Grandma, family members called me "Grandma's shadow." She told me many stories about the years when she was a little girl, a young wife, and mother. She said she was born in San Lorenzo and often talked about "Eden."

— *Tilli Holm Calhoun*

Recipes marked with this Danish flower icon are from Ida's kitchen.

Carl Holm's parents,
Carl Emile Holm, Sr.
and "Minnie" Holm

Carl and Ida Holm in Santa Cruz

Back, left to right: Chris Madsen, Chris Fredricksen,
Chris Sankenburg, "Monkey Face" Jonhson
Front, left to right: Hans Madsen, "Butcher" Madison,
Carl Holm

Carl and Ida Holm
with their first child,
Walter

Leslie, Gladys, Dick, and Ida Holm
on a buckboard with Dora Jessen
Rasmussen in the background, 1905

Back, left to right:
Gladys Holm, Ida Jessen
Holm, Annie Tretzel;
Front, left to right:
Sophie Jorgensen Holm,
Mabel Holm Jorgensen,
Bertha Holm Brown,
Elvira Holm (Ida's
granddaughter)

Fair View

The Holm family inspecting their new home, 1905
Back: Carl, Walter, Ida, and Mabel
Middle: Leslie, Dick, Bertha, and Art
Front: Gladys

The crew of Danish "squarehead" carpenters painting the house

Rear view

The dining room on the Farm (Elvira Holm's baby shower circa 1940s)

The "Little House" at Fair View, which was built before the main house. The previous owner, Jacob Hardy, lived here before selling the property to Carl Holm in 1891. The builder, Mr. Andersen, lived in the "Little House" while constructing the "fine new cottage." Mona and Les Holm are pictured here.

13

Warner Wilbur Holm **Family History**

On November 28, 1900, Warner Wilbur Holm was born, the ninth and last of Carl and Ida Holm's children. He was named Warner Wilbur after a well-respected doctor in the Livermore Valley. At that time, Carl and Ida lived and farmed on the area that is now the Stoneridge Mall and business park in Pleasanton, California.

Warner "Dick" Wilbur Holm. He was called "Papa" by his many grandchildren.

Warner never liked his given name. When one of his brothers jokingly started calling him Dick, after a family horse, he was happy to make it stick long after the horse died.

When Dick was six years old, the family moved to their new home, Fair View, located in Livermore on the south side of Stanley Boulevard, east of Isabel Avenue. He attended the Fifth Street School and went on to study at Livermore High School for two years. Dick then enrolled at Heald Business College. Upon his graduation, he declined a bank's offer of employment, as he knew working the land was his passion.

Although Dick was the baby of the family and enjoyed some of the advantages of that position, he learned to work hard from the time he was quite young; it was necessary for everyone to pitch in on the farm in those days. The work was hard, but he loved the freshness of the morning, the richness of plowed earth, the sweetness of new grass, and the new foals, lambs, and calves.

During the great flu epidemic of 1918, Dick contracted the dreaded disease and barely survived. Many people in the valley did die. He saw many sick and recalled seeing the bodies of those not as fortunate as he being hauled away in wagons.

Dick went into farming with his brother Les, on land they rented from their father. Together they formed the Holm Bros. ranching enterprise and created the Circle H as their livestock brand. As their business grew, they leased more land and in the 1920s acquired acreage of their own on Mines Road at about $5 an acre. Over the years, they raised grain, hay, horses, sheep, cattle, grapes, and walnuts.

Dick Holm (center) with (clockwise from upper right) Tilli, Jimmy, Patsy, Richie, and Frank

Dick married Ione Teeter, a longtime acquaintance, on March 31, 1926, in her grandmother's home in Alameda. The family started in earnest when the twins, Merilyn and Frank, were born on April Fools' Day of 1929. James followed in February of 1933, Richard in June of 1935, and Patsy in November of 1936.

Dick used to say that the mustard weed in a farmer's field was a measure of his laziness, so one of the children's earliest chores was pulling out the mustard. From there, they went on to gathering eggs, picking walnuts, grapes, and other crops, milking cows, herding cattle, and anything that needed some extra hands. When his grandchildren came along, he kept them busy by paying them a quarter for each tomato hornworm removed from his tomato plants and for each bucket of rocks removed from his vegetable garden.

Dick took great pride in his farming and his diligence was obvious in the quality of his commodities. He loved his work, especially the work he did with his team of horses. He could be seen grading the streets of downtown Livermore with his horses before the streets were paved and continued to use them to plow on the farm long after tractors became standard.

Dick was not a stern introvert like his father, but an outgoing, fun-lover like his mother. He loved to play with and tease his children. When grandchildren and great-grandchildren arrived, he expressed his playfulness, lighthearted teasing, and love to them all. He was blessed with nine grandchildren: Gary, Susan, David, Merry, Wendy, Peggy, Lori, Nancy, and Jimmy, who loved to spend time with "Papa." They knew when they were with him, they would be sure to have an adventure.

In 1966, Dick and Ione built a home on the Mines Road property and lived there for the rest of their lives. When Dick retired from ranching in the 1970's, he continued to raise much of their own food by growing a huge, productive and beautiful vegetable garden and raising pigeons. Red onions were his specialty and visitors to his home during the summer would usually leave with a large red onion or two.

The Livermore community benefited from Dick Holm's efforts, as well. As a trustee for the Livermore Elementary School District, he worked hard to increase the salaries of teachers and to start a music program. He served on the committee that raised money to fund Valley Memorial Hospital. He was also an active member of the Alameda County Farm Bureau, California Cattlemen's Association, Native Sons of the Golden West, the Presbyterian Church, and the Dania Lodge of Livermore.

Dick loved traveling. Often through his Farm Bureau connections, he journeyed throughout Europe, Australia, and New Zealand. He saw much of the United States, including Alaska and Hawaii. When Gary Holm, his first grandchild, was born in Tennessee, Dick went a-travelling to see him.

Dick Holm passed away in 1986 at the age of eighty-five while working outside in his beloved garden.

Ione and her mother, Hattie circa 1906

Ione Teeter Holm **Family History**

Ione's roots in the Livermore Valley began when her grandfather Daniel Teeter and his brother, Jacob, headed west from Arkansas in the 1850s. They were members of a drive bringing cattle to feed the gold seekers who were flooding California. Jacob became the first blacksmith in Pleasanton, but he later returned to Arkansas.

In 1870, Daniel married Caroline Arnett from Sunol, California, a native of Madison County, Missouri, and settled on a farm on Arroyo Road in Livermore. Daniel became a prominent farmer with a threshing crew that toured the valley during harvest times. The Teeters' son, Frank (Ione's father), was born on February 2, 1878. Caroline died of "consumption" in 1882, leaving Frank and his sister Flora. She was buried on Oak Knoll with three of her babies, on a site where the Teeter farm could be seen. Daniel later remarried a woman named Susan Braly.

In the early 1900s, Frank traveled to Arkansas to visit his father's family, where he met and married a pretty young school teacher named Hattie Puntney. Ione was their first child, born on February 23, 1906, followed by Gray, Reba, and Ed. When Ione was young, the family lived on the Stanley Farm on North Livermore Avenue. Hattie became ill in 1917 when Ione was 11 years old. Frank and his family brought Hattie by train to her parent's home in Monticello, Arkansas, where she died and was buried.

The Daniel Teeter family. Daniel is in the back row (center) with hat and beard; Gray and Ed Teeter are in the middle row, third and fourth from the left. On their right are Reba and Ione Teeter with Aunt Dixie; Dan's wife, Susie Braly Teeter, is in the back row, fourth from left, holding a baby.

Returning to California, Frank and the children lived on the Teeter farm on Arroyo Road. Frank was in the construction business and built many homes in Livermore, which included the Volponi home on Fourth and O Streets, the Baxter home on Rincon Avenue, the McLain home on Wente Street, and the Lyon home on Livermore Avenue. Frank enrolled the children at the Livermore Grammar School on Fifth Street (which Ione's children and grandchildren later attended). Ione thought her teacher, Vera Crane, was quite a romantic figure, wearing a bouquet of violets on her neckline.

Ione passed away in 1998 at the age of ninety-one in her home on Mines Road with family members by her side.

Recipes marked with this Danish flower icon are from Ione's kitchen.

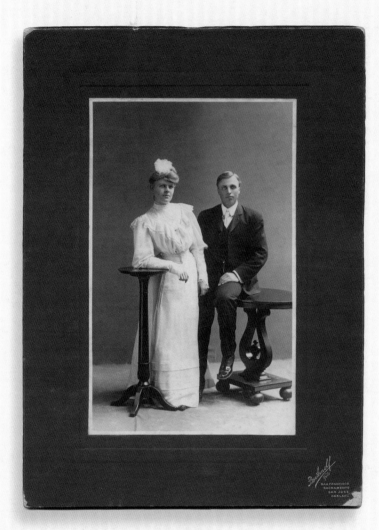

Walter Holm with his bride, Annie Tretzel Holm
February 22, 1906

Don, Ray, and Howard Tretzel
with baby Lowell Holm,
circa 1915

Annie Holm and baby Elvira

Christian, Catherine, Carl, and Eric Holm

Elvira Lillian Holm,
three years old

Elvira Holm

Skinnies (Jam–Filled Pancakes)

Makes 2 servings

When we used to go pheasant hunting at Hazel and Andy Oliver's ranch, Hazel would make us these pancakes, which are kind of like crêpes. On Sundays, my father, Stanley Jorgensen, would also occasionally make them for us. Throughout the years, as my family grew, I also made skinnies every once in a while. Now when my children Cindy and Andrew come home, we have to have them.

CARL JORGENSEN *from Hazel Oliver, Edna Jorgensen's sister*

Stanley Jorgensen

3 eggs
½ cup flour
1 teaspoon sugar
½ teaspoon salt
1 cup milk
1 tablespoon butter or shortening plus more for oiling the pan
Jam, syrup, or other fillings of your choice

Preheat the oven to 150°F. In a bowl, beat the eggs until frothy. Add the flour, sugar, and salt and mix well. Add the milk and butter and continue mixing until thin and very smooth. Melt enough butter in a 9-inch or 10-inch skillet to coat the bottom. Pour 4 to 5 tablespoons of batter into the hot skillet. Turn and slant the pan to spread the batter into a very thin pancake. Cook until browned, then turn and cook the other side. Slip the pancakes onto a warming platter and put the platter into the warm oven until ready to serve; this will soften them up. To serve, put some jam, syrup, or other filling on each pancake and roll them loosely with a fork. Serve immediately.

Edna Jorgensen at
Santa Cruz

Carter Christmas Breakfast

*Before we had kids that woke us at 4:00 a.m. on Christmas morning to open gifts, Darrell and I hosted Christmas breakfast for several years. As guests arrived, they were served Peach Mimosas (page 39). In addition to fresh fruit and the Calhoun family's traditional linguisa, I would serve Raelene Vieux's **Potato and Ham Bake Breakfast Special**, **Butterscotch Breakfast Rolls**, and **Pumpkin Apple Streusel Muffins**. The recipes for these three dishes are on these pages.*

—Merry Carter

Clockwise from left front: Darrell Carter, Wayne Calhoun, Tilli Calhoun, Marilyn Carter, and Donald Carter

Potato and Ham Bake Breakfast Special *Serves 6*

This recipe was given to me and my sister, Susie Calhoun, by Raelene Vieux. The Vieux family were local cattle ranchers who were used to serving meals to many people. You can double the recipe to serve twelve people—use a 9- by 13-inch baking dish. When I make this dish, I use hash brown patties and omit the butter.

Merry "Lambie" Calhoun Carter

½ (30-ounce) package frozen hash browns, thawed
¼ cup (½ stick) butter, melted
1½ cups diced ham
½ (4-ounce) can chopped green chilies, drained
½ cup shredded Monterey Jack cheese (about 2 ounces)
½ cup shredded Cheddar cheese (about 2 ounces)
2 eggs
⅔ cup half-and-half

Preheat the oven to 425°F. Line a 12-inch pie pan or an 8- by 8-inch baking dish with the thawed hash browns, pressing them firmly into the bottom and up the sides of the pan as you would when making a graham cracker pie crust. Pour the butter around the edges. (If using patties, omit this step.) Bake for 20 minutes or until crispy. Remove from the oven and arrange the ham, chilies, and cheeses in layers on the browned crust.

In a small bowl, whisk together the eggs and half-and-half and pour the mixture over the layers. Bake for 30 minutes or until golden and an inserted knife comes out clean.

Raelene and Don Vieux

Butterscotch Breakfast Rolls

Makes 24 rolls

MERRY "LAMBIE" CALHOUN CARTER from Becky Calhoun Foster

1 cup chopped pecans

1 package frozen uncooked dinner roll dough (24 rolls), thawed

1 (3.4-ounce) box butterscotch pudding mix

1 cup brown sugar

½ cup (1 stick) butter, melted

Spray a 10-inch Bundt pan or angel food cake pan with oil or butter. Sprinkle in the pecans and arrange the rolls on top of them. In a small bowl, combine the pudding mix and brown sugar. Sprinkle the mixture over the rolls and drizzle with the melted butter. Cover with plastic wrap and let rise in the refrigerator overnight. In the morning, preheat the oven to 350°F. Bake for 30 to 40 minutes or until golden.

To serve, invert on a large platter.

Pumpkin-Apple Streusel Muffins

Makes 18 muffins

MERRY "LAMBIE" CALHOUN CARTER

Streusel topping

2 tablespoons flour

¼ cup sugar

½ teaspoon ground cinnamon

¼ cup (½ stick) butter plus more for oiling the muffin tins

Muffins

2½ cups all-purpose flour

2 cups granulated sugar

1 tablespoon pumpkin pie spice

1 teaspoon baking soda

½ teaspoon salt

2 eggs, lightly beaten

1 cup canned pumpkin

½ cup vegetable oil

2 cups peeled, finely chopped apples

In a small bowl combine the flour, sugar, and cinnamon. Cut in the butter with a pastry blender or 2 knives until the mixture has a crumbly texture. Set aside.

Preheat the oven to 350°F. Butter two 12-cup muffin tins or line them with paper liners. In a large mixing bowl, combine the flour, sugar, pumpkin pie spice, baking soda, and salt; set aside. In a medium-sized bowl, combine the eggs, pumpkin, and oil. Add the liquid ingredients to the dry ingredients and stir until just moistened. Stir in the apples and spoon the batter into the muffin cups, filling them ¾ full. Sprinkle streusel topping over the batter. Bake for 35 to 40 minutes or until an inserted toothpick comes out clean.

French Toast for a Crowd

Serves 6

I like to make this recipe for Christmas morning—it's yummy!

Gayle Fachner Diltz

12 slices white or sourdough bread
¾ pound cream cheese cut into 6 slices
½ cup sugar, divided
12 eggs
⅓ cup maple syrup plus more for serving
1 teaspoon almond extract
2 cups milk

Remove the crusts from the bread. Place 6 slices in the bottom of a nonreactive 3-quart baking dish. Arrange the cream cheese slices on top of the bread. Sprinkle ¼ cup of the sugar over the cream cheese. Top with the remaining bread. Beat together the eggs, syrup, almond extract, and milk. Pour the mixture over the bread and sprinkle with the remaining sugar. Cover and refrigerate overnight. When you are getting ready to eat, preheat the oven to 375°F and bake the French toast mixture for 1 hour or until puffed and golden brown. Serve with warm maple syrup on the side.

Sheepherder's Potatoes

Serves 4

Merry "Lambie" Calhoun Carter

6 medium-sized yellow or red potatoes
2 tablespoons olive oil
¾ cup chopped yellow onions
6 slices cooked bacon, crumbled
4 eggs
2 tablespoons milk
2 tablespoons chopped fresh parsley
¼ teaspoon salt
⅛ teaspoon pepper

Boil the potatoes in a pot until almost tender, about 35 minutes. When they are cool enough to handle, cut crosswise into ⅛-inch slices. Set aside.

Preheat the oven to 375°F. In a large oven-proof skillet over medium heat, add the oil and sauté the onions until softened but not brown, about 7 minutes. Carefully add the potato slices and gently toss with the onions and about ¾ of the crumbled bacon. Shake the pan until the potatoes lie in a thick, flat layer. Cover and cook until the bottom of the layer is golden brown, about 15 to 20 minutes.

Meanwhile, in a medium-sized bowl, beat the eggs with the milk, parsley, salt, and pepper. Pour the egg mixture over the potatoes and sprinkle the remaining bacon on top. Place the skillet in the oven and bake until the eggs are set, about 8 to 10 minutes.

Williamsburg Soufflé

Serves 8

My mother, Gayle Diltz, gave me this recipe. I remember her making it on Christmas morning along with the usual things—juice, coffee, and fruit. The whole family would feast while opening presents or watching the little ones rip open their packages. It has become a tradition that I hope to pass along to my four children. I vary the flavors in this soufflé depending on my mood and what's in the refrigerator. You can substitute Monterey Jack cheese, green chilies, and hot sausage for the sausage and Cheddar cheese.

KORINNE DILTZ

8 slices day-old white or sourdough bread

¼ cup (½ stick) butter or margarine plus more for oiling the baking dish

2 cups sliced fresh mushrooms or 1 (12-ounce) can, drained

1 cup minced yellow onions

2 cups cooked, crumbled sausage

8 eggs

2 tablespoons flour

2 tablespoons prepared mustard

2 cups half-and-half

4 cups shredded Cheddar cheese (about 1 pound)

1 tablespoon garlic salt

Trim the crusts from the bread and cut it into bite-size pieces. Generously butter a 13- x 9-inch baking dish and arrange the bread in the bottom. In a skillet over medium heat, melt the butter and sauté the mushrooms and onions for 5 minutes. Spoon the mixture over the bread and top with the cooked sausage. Beat the eggs in a bowl and add the flour, mustard, half-and-half, cheese, and garlic salt, and blend well. Pour the egg mixture over the sausage, cover, and refrigerate for at least 4 hours or overnight.

Preheat the oven to 325°F. Bake the soufflé, uncovered, for 1 hour or until golden and puffy. Serve immediately.

The Diltz family: Don, Gayle, Kristine, Korinne, Dylan Serrano, and Kevin Avila

Wedding of Gayle Fachner and Don Diltz, 1965

Aebleskivers (Danish Ball Pancakes) Makes 12 aebleskivers

This recipe was given to me by my dad, Stanley Jorgensen, who always made aebleskivers at Christmastime. Now we make them for our grandchildren on Christmas morning because they were one of our children's favorites. Aebleskivers are cooked over medium heat on the stove in a special aebleskiver pan.

CAROL JORGENSEN MILLER

3 eggs, separated
2 tablespoons sugar
½ teaspoon salt
2 cups buttermilk
2 cups flour
½ teaspoon baking soda
1 teaspoon baking powder
Butter for oiling the pan
Applesauce, nuts, jam, raisins or
    other fillings
Maple syrup, jam, or powdered sugar
    for serving

Beat the egg yolks in a medium-sized bowl. Add the sugar, salt, and buttermilk and mix well. Sift together the flour, soda, and baking powder and combine them with the egg mixture. In another bowl, beat the egg whites until stiff. Gently fold them into the egg-flour mixture.

Heat the aebleskiver pan over medium heat and butter it, being careful not to burn yourself. The batter will sizzle when added. Fill each hole of the pan ⅔ full. Cook until bubbling, then add a tablespoon of applesauce or other fillings on top of each one. Turn the aebleskivers with a fork or small knitting needle and cook the other side until medium brown. Serve with butter and maple syrup or jam, or generously sprinkle with powdered sugar.

John Wayne Casserole Serves 8

This recipe came from my mom, "Mimi." She used to serve it at breakfast on Easter Sunday. Don't use jalapeños for the chilies!

CAROL HOLM NEWMAN

Butter for oiling the pan
2 (4-ounce) cans chopped green chilies
¾ pound Monterey Jack cheese, shredded
¾ pound sharp Cheddar cheese, shredded
4 eggs, separated
⅔ cup evaporated milk
1 tablespoon flour
1 teaspoon salt

Preheat the oven to 350°F. Butter a 9- by 13-inch baking dish. In a bowl, combine the chilies and cheese and put them in the pan. Beat the egg whites in a clean bowl, until they form soft peaks. In another bowl, combine the egg yolks with the milk, flour, and salt. Gently fold the egg whites into the yolk mixture. Pour the egg mixture over the cheese mixture and gently stir until blended. Bake for 30 minutes or until golden and an inserted knife comes out clean.

Scotch Scones

BOBBIE LIVERMORE BAIRD

⅔ cup cold butter or margarine plus
    more for oiling the baking sheet
1 egg
¾ cup milk
3 cups flour
⅔ cup sugar
1 tablespoon baking powder
½ teaspoon salt
⅔ cup currants or other dried fruit,
    chopped into small pieces

Preheat the oven to 425°F. Lightly butter a baking sheet. In a small bowl, beat the egg with a fork and blend in the milk. In another bowl, combine the flour, sugar, baking powder, and salt. Cut in the shortening as you would when making a pie crust, blending the ingredients until they resemble coarse cornmeal. Add the currants. Add the egg-milk mixture in small amounts, stirring with a fork until the dough just begins to hold together. Knead the dough a few times and divide it into 3 rounds. Pat out each round on a floured board or piece of waxed paper until it is about ½ inch thick. Cut the dough into diamond shapes, place on the baking sheet about 1 inch apart, and bake for 12 to 15 minutes or until golden and an inserted toothpick comes out clean.

"Darn Goods" (Cinnamon-Sugar Puffs) *Makes about 1 dozen*

My sister and I would make these when we were young with our mom's help.

WENDY NEELY HOWE

Oil for deep fat frying
¼ cup sugar
1 teaspoon ground cinnamon
1 cup Bisquick baking mix
¼ cup cold water

Pour the oil into a skillet to a depth of 1½ inches and heat to 375°F. Mix the sugar and cinnamon together in a paper or plastic bag. In a bowl, blend the Bisquick and water together to form a soft dough. Drop rounded teaspoonfuls of dough into the hot fat and fry about half a minute on each side or until golden brown and puffy. Remove from the oil and drain on a plate lined with paper towels. While still warm, place the puffs in the bag and shake in the sugar mixture to lightly coat.

Fresh Fruit Soup

There is a classic Danish fruit soup recipe called *sødsuppe* that uses dried fruit, usually prunes and raisins. It was flavored with fruit juices such as cherry, plum, or any other red juice. This is our California version, which calls for fresh fruit instead. It may sound like a strange concoction, but it is delicious, and so refreshing.

JOANNE KAMP

5½ cups water
⅔ cup quick-cooking tapioca
¼ cup sugar
Dash of salt
1 (16-ounce) can frozen orange juice
2 peaches, peeled and sliced
2 oranges, peeled and chopped
2 bananas, sliced
1 cup seedless grapes
1 cup fresh strawberries, sliced
2 tablespoons freshly squeezed lemon juice

In a pot over high heat, combine 3 cups of the water, the tapioca, sugar, and salt. Bring to a full rolling boil, stirring constantly. Pour the mixture into a large bowl, add the frozen orange juice, and stir until melted. Add the remaining 2½ cups water, stir, and cool for 40 minutes. Stir, cover, and chill for 3 hours or overnight. Stir in the fruit and lemon juice just before serving. The soup will be slightly thickened.

The Kamps, good friends of Ida and Carl Holm

Ida Holm and Hansine Kamp

A Soup Story In 1856, Hans Nicolaysen Kempt was born in Denmark and came to America when he was sixteen. Upon arriving, he changed his name from Kempt to Kamp. He met Hansine Lausten while living in the Livermore area and they married in 1880. Hans joined the Dania Society where he and Hansine became close friends with Carl and Ida Holm, starting a friendship that would last through generations. The Kamps purchased property on Tassajara Road, where they raised their twelve children. Hans opened Kamps Furniture in Livermore in 1904, and the family ran the business for ninety years. Their oldest son, Hans, had two children, Harold and Eleanor, who were born on their grandparents' ranch. Harold married Frances Johnson, and they had two children, Russell and Karen. Russ became good friends with Carl Holm, great-grandson of Ida, who was an attendant in Russ's wedding. Russ and his wife, Joanne, still reside in Livermore, and their children Laura, David, Heather, and Chris are good friends of Nancy Mueller, Ida Holm's great-grand-daughter. Nancy attended a brunch hosted by Joanne and Heather, and that is how this recipe came to be, a California version of *sødsuppe*, the traditional Danish cold fruit soup.

Gary and Jeri, sitting in a tree, k-i-s-s-i-n-g. First comes Love, then comes Marriage...
It all began in 1971, the very first time Ione Holm's first grandson, Gary, set eyes upon Jeri Sveen in the 300 hall of Livermore's Granada High School. By the following fall, Gary was spending most of his free time at the Sveen household. Intrigued by the Navy career of Jerry Sveen, Jeri Sveen's father, he soon signed up—beginning more than twenty-four years of military service. Marriage came next, followed by the arrival of Brett and Derek. From Hawaii, to Scotland, to the American Southeast, the family lived away from the Livermore area the entire length of Gary's naval career. However, strong family ties always brought them back. Many reunions found them up with "Grandma in the hills," as she was lovingly referred to by Brett and Derek. Ione Holm kept the Holm and Sveen clans drawn together with her love of family. To this day, the two families enjoy a warm and loving relationship. All who knew Ione loved her open heart and welcoming spirit.

—Jeri Sveen Holm

Breakfast Casserole

Serves 8 to 12

This recipe came from my cousin in Chicago. She served it at a family reunion that took us all to Illinois in 1989. I've made it on many occasions since, including a few Mother's Day brunches. It's easy and good.

POLLY SVEEN GALLAGHER

Butter for oiling the pan
1 (6-ounce) box onion and garlic croutons
1 (16-ounce) package Jimmy Dean pork sausage, browned
2½ cups shredded Cheddar cheese (about 10 ounces)
4 eggs
1 cup plus ½ cup milk
½ teaspoon dry mustard
1 (10.75-ounce) can cream of mushroom soup
1 (30-ounce) package frozen hash brown potatoes, thawed
Salt and pepper

The night before you want to serve the casserole, butter a 13- by 9- by 2-inch casserole dish. Spread half the croutons in the bottom and cover them with a layer of half the sausage and 1 cup of the cheese. Repeat, using the remaining croutons, sausage, and cheese. In a mixing bowl, combine the eggs, 1 cup of the milk, and mustard, and pour over the layered ingredients. Cover and refrigerate overnight.

In the morning, preheat the oven to 325°F. In a small bowl, combine the soup and the remaining ½ cup of milk, and pour over the layered ingredients. Evenly cover with the potatoes, season with salt and pepper to taste, and sprinkle with the remaining cup of cheese. Bake uncovered for 1½ hours or until an inserted toothpick comes out clean.

Mother's Day, 2004
The Sveen family: Brenda, Kristi, Rae, Jerry, Jeri, Polly, and Donny

Sausage and Eggs

Becky Calhoun Foster

Serves 4

Butter for oiling the pan
8 slices white bread, crusts removed, cubed
2 cups shredded sharp Cheddar cheese
 (about ½ pound)
1½ pounds link sausages, cut into fourths
4 eggs
¾ teaspoon dry mustard
2¼ cups milk
1 can cream of mushroom soup

The night before you serve this dish, butter an 8- by 12-inch casserole. Place the cubed bread in the bottom of the casserole and top with the cheese. In a skillet over medium-high heat, brown the sausage. Drain and spread evenly over the cheese. In a bowl, beat the eggs, add the dry mustard, milk, and soup, and combine well. Pour this mixture over the cheese-sausage mixture, and refrigerate overnight.

When ready to serve, preheat the oven to 300°F. Bake for 1½ hours or until an inserted toothpick comes out clean. Cool slightly to set.

Breakfast Sausage Pudding

Vickie Regnolds Warden

Serves 8

Butter for oiling the pan
12 slices white bread, crusts removed,
 buttered
½ cup (1 stick) butter
2½ cups sliced fresh mushrooms
2 cups sliced yellow onions
1½ pounds mild ground Italian sausage
1 pound Cheddar cheese, shredded
5 eggs
2½ cups milk
3 teaspoons Dijon mustard
1 teaspoon dry mustard
1 teaspoon grated nutmeg
2 tablespoons chopped fresh parsley

Butter a 13- by 9-inch casserole.

Melt the butter in a skillet over medium-high heat. Add the mushrooms and onions and sauté until soft, 5 to 7 minutes. In another skillet, brown the sausage, breaking it into small bits.

Lay half of the bread on the bottom of the casserole, then cover with half the mushroom mixture, sausage, and cheese. Add another layer of bread and cover with layers of the remaining mushroom mixture, sausage, and cheese, in that order.

In a bowl, beat together the eggs and milk. Add the Dijon mustard, dry mustard, nutmeg, and parsley. Mix well and pour over the layers. Cover and refrigerate overnight.

When ready to serve, preheat the oven to 350°F, and bake the casserole, uncovered, for 1 hour or until an inserted toothpick comes out clean.

Spinach Sausage Pie

BECKY CALHOUN FOSTER

Pie dough for 2 (9-inch) double-crust pies
1 pound Italian sausage links, chopped
6 eggs
2 (10-ounce) packages frozen chopped spinach, thawed, drained, and squeezed to remove moisture
1 pound mozzarella cheese, shredded (about 4 cups)
1 cup ricotta cheese
1 teaspoon salt
⅛ teaspoon pepper
⅛ teaspoon garlic powder

Preheat the oven to 375°F and line the bottoms of two 9-inch pie plates with dough.

In a skillet over medium-high heat, brown the sausage and drain off the fat. Separate 1 egg and set the egg yolk aside. In a large bowl, beat the egg white with the other 5 eggs. Mix in the spinach, both cheeses, salt, pepper, and garlic powder. Add the sausage and combine well.

Roll out the dough for the top crusts of the pies, cutting several slits in each of them to let the steam escape. Set aside the leftover scraps. Fill each pie with half of the sausage-egg filling. Top each pie with a round of dough and crimp the edges. Make decorative leaves with the leftover dough and arrange them around the center of the pies. In a small bowl, whisk together the egg yolk and 1 tablespoon water; brush the tops of the pies with the mixture. Bake for 1 hour and 15 minutes—the crust should be a light golden brown and the egg mixture set in the center when done.

New Joe's Special

This recipe comes from the old New Joe's Restaurant in San Francisco's North Beach. It's good for a quick dinner or brunch anytime.

VIVIAN BRIZEE CALHOUN

1 pound hamburger
1 medium yellow onion, chopped
3 cloves garlic, minced
2 cups sliced fresh mushrooms
1 (10-ounce) package frozen chopped spinach, thawed, drained, and squeezed to remove the moisture
5 eggs (or Eggbeaters)
Salt and pepper

In a skillet over medium-high heat, add the hamburger, onion, and garlic and sauté until the meat is browned. Add the mushrooms and cook until soft. Mix in the spinach. In a small bowl, beat the eggs and season with salt and pepper to taste. Stir continuously while slowly adding the eggs. Cook until the eggs are set, stirring constantly.

Bacon Spinach Casserole

Yes, this recipe uses eighteen eggs!

PEGGY HOLM RENNICK

1 tablespoon butter plus more for oiling
    the casserole
1 cup fresh mushrooms, sliced
18 eggs
2 cups milk
1½ pounds bacon, cooked and crumbled
3 cups shredded Cheddar cheese
    (about ¾ pound)
1 (10-ounce) package frozen chopped
    spinach, thawed and drained
1 small yellow onion, chopped
3 cups Cheddar cheese croutons

Preheat the oven to 325°F. Butter a 9- by 12-inch casserole.

In a frying pan over medium-high heat, melt the butter. Add the mushrooms and brown, 3 to 5 minutes. Set aside.

In a large mixing bowl, whisk together the eggs. Add the milk and whisk together. Add the mushrooms, bacon, cheese, spinach, and onion, and mix well. Pour the mixture into the casserole and layer the croutons on top. Bake, uncovered, for 1 hour or until set. Let cool for 10 minutes.

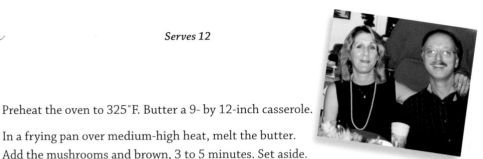

*Peggy Holm Rennick and
Mike Rennick*

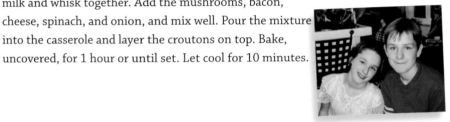

Molly and Colin Rennick

Eggs Fantastic

BECKY CALHOUN FOSTER

9 eggs
1 cup sour cream
1 large yellow onion, chopped
1 cup sliced fresh mushrooms
1 pound Jimmy Dean sausage, crumbled
¾ cup prepared salsa
1 cup shredded Cheddar cheese
1 cup shredded Monterey Jack cheese
1 cup shredded mozzarella cheese
4 ounces sliced Velveeta cheese

Preheat the oven to 400°F and butter a 9- by 13-inch baking dish. In a blender, combine the eggs and sour cream; blend until smooth. Pour the mixture into the baking dish and bake for 6 to 8 minutes, or until set; cool.

Reduce the oven temperature to 325°F. In a skillet over medium heat, sauté the onion, mushrooms, and sausage until the sausage is no longer pink. Drain off any excess fat. Spread the salsa over the baked egg mixture, and sprinkle the sausage mixture on top. Sprinkle with the cheeses and cover with the Velveeta slices. Bake for 20 to 25 minutes or until the cheese is melted.

Remembering Dick and Ione

The green playroom at the old house on Stanley Boulevard
Grandma's jellies and preserves
The Fourth of July barbecues
The deer barbecues
The many dinners Grandma made for the cowboys
The cold, wet days by the fireplace
Grandma being there to listen to us
Grandma's birthday dinners at the Claremont Hotel and Croce's
The Salinas Rodeo and picnic and the Grand National Rodeo
Grandma enjoying playing cards
Cedar Mountain and the many birds and animals we'd see there
Our many Christmases together
Grandpa's garden of vegetables
Grandma's warm hand on my head when things weren't going right
The rodeo parades and lunch after at Tilli's
The Pleasanton parades and Dean's Cafe
The horseback rides up and down the hills
Grandma's perfume bottles upstairs at the old house
The kindness and endless love that Grandma and Grandpa gave to us and to so many others

—Dave Holm

Pineapple Muffins

Makes 18 muffins

I have made these muffins for many brunches. The pineapple adds a little sparkle.

BECKY CALHOUN FOSTER

Butter for oiling the pan
2 cups flour
½ teaspoon salt
3 teaspoons baking powder
¼ teaspoon grated nutmeg
½ teaspoon ground cinnamon
¼ cup softened shortening
½ cup sugar
1 egg, beaten
1 cup milk
1 cup drained, crushed pineapple
Powdered sugar and ground cinnamon for sprinkling
3 tablespoons butter, melted

Preheat the oven to 375°F and butter two 10-cup muffin tins.

Sift together the flour, salt, baking powder, nutmeg, and cinnamon. In a bowl, cream together the shortening and sugar; blend in the egg. Add ½ cup or so of the dry ingredients to the shortening mixture, and then beat in about ¼ cup of the milk. Alternately add the dry ingredients and the milk until everything is well combined. Fold in the pineapple.

Fill the muffin tins half full with the batter. Lightly sprinkle the top of each muffin with powdered sugar and cinnamon. Bake for 15 minutes, or until an inserted toothpick comes out clean.

Remove the muffins from the oven, dust again with powdered sugar and cinnamon, and drizzle ½ teaspoon melted butter over each muffin. Return to the oven and bake for 1 minute more.

Kona Banana Bread

GLADYS BRIZEE

Makes two 9- by 5-inch loaves

Butter for oiling the pan

2 cups sugar

1 cup butter or shortening

2 cups mashed ripe bananas (about 4 bananas)

4 eggs, well beaten

2½ cups flour

¼ teaspoon salt

2 teaspoons baking soda

2 cups chopped nuts

Preheat the oven to 350°F and butter two 9- by 5-inch loaf tins.

In a mixing bowl, cream together the sugar and shortening. Blend in the bananas, eggs, flour, salt, and baking soda. Fold in the nuts. Do not over mix. Bake for 50 to 55 minutes on the middle rack, then lower the heat to 250°F. Continue baking for an additional 10 minutes or until an inserted toothpick comes out clean.

Zucchini Bread

SUSIE CALHOUN with help from Mildred McCune

Makes two 9- by 5-inch loaves

1 cup vegetable oil plus more for oiling the pan

3 eggs

2 cups sugar

1½ cups nuts

3 cups flour

1 teaspoon salt

1 teaspoon baking soda

1 teaspoon ground cinnamon

¼ teaspoon baking powder

2 or 3 cups shredded zucchini

Preheat the oven to 350°F and oil and flour two 9- by 5-inch loaf pans.

In a mixing bowl, beat together the eggs, oil, and sugar. In another bowl, combine the nuts, flour, salt, baking soda, cinnamon, and baking powder. Blend the dry ingredients into the egg mixture; then add the zucchini and stir until combined. Bake for 1 hour, or until an inserted toothpick comes out clean.

Killer Cheese Bread

Serves 12

This recipe was given to me by my teaching partner and excellent hostess, Sue Mears. I first brought this delicacy to Easter in the hills and everyone loved it. You can freeze this bread after it is assembled and wrapped in foil. Defrost it before you bake it.

SUSIE CALHOUN

1 cup (2 sticks) melted butter
1 tablespoon lemon juice
1 tablespoon Dijon mustard
1 (2.8-ounce) package Good Seasons
    Italian Dressing seasoning mix
1 large round sourdough French bread
1 pound Swiss or Monterey Jack cheese
    (or any combination), shredded

Preheat the oven to 350°F. In a bowl, mix together the butter, lemon juice, mustard, and Italian dressing mix. Cut a ½-inch slice off the bottom of the bread and place it on a large sheet of aluminum foil. Cut the remaining bread into cubes by cutting the loaf first horizontally, then longitudinally, then vertically. Carefully keep the slices together in the shape of the loaf as you cut them into cubes. You will end up with a cubed loaf of bread that still retains the original loaf shape. Place the cubed loaf on top of the bottom slice. Pull the edges of the foil up around the cubes to keep them in place. Stuff the crevices between the cubes with cheese and pour the butter mixture over all. Cover tightly with another sheet of foil, and bake for 45 minutes or until heated through and the cheese is bubbling.

Garlic Bread

Serves 24

I often bring this garlic bread to potlucks and get-togethers. I prepare the bread at home and bring the foil-wrapped loaves with me, then heat them upon arrival.

SUE KILGO BOIES

3 loaves of good crusty French bread
1½ cups (3 sticks) butter, softened
Cloves from 1 garlic head, separated,
    peeled, and minced

Preheat the oven to 450°F. In a small bowl, cream together the softened butter and minced garlic. Cut the loaves in half lengthwise and slather them with the garlic butter. Wrap the loaves in heavy-duty aluminum foil and place them in the oven for 20 to 30 minutes, or until heated through.

Persimmon Nut Bread

Makes 1 9- by 5-inch loaf

Use persimmons that are very ripe and soft—the fruit is easily scooped out of the skins and ready to use in this recipe.

BOBBIE LIVERMORE BAIRD

Bob and Nada Livermore
(Bobbie Baird's parents)

½ cup (1 stick) margarine plus
    more for oiling the pan

2 cups sifted flour

1 teaspoon ground cinnamon

1 teaspoon baking powder

½ teaspoon grated nutmeg

1 teaspoon baking soda

½ teaspoon ground cloves

½ teaspoon salt

2 eggs, beaten

¾ cup sugar

1 teaspoon vanilla extract

1 cup persimmon pulp (2 to 3 persimmons)

½ cup walnuts

½ cup raisins

Eighth Grade Graduating Class 1943

Bobbie Livermore, Tilli, and
Frank Holm went to kindergarten
through twelfth grade together

Preheat the oven to 350°F and generously butter a 9- by 5-inch loaf pan.

In a bowl, sift together the flour, cinnamon, baking powder, nutmeg, baking soda, cloves, and salt. In another mixing bowl, cream together the margarine, eggs, sugar, and vanilla. Gradually blend the flour mixture into the egg mixture. Add the pulp, walnuts, and raisins and mix. Pour the batter into the loaf pan and bake for 55 to 60 minutes or until an inserted toothpick comes out clean.

Left to right: Nancy Henry, Audrey
Forney, Tilli Holm, Bobbie Livermore,
and Leona Fehrenbach at Merrill
Groth's birthday party

A family reunion at Art Holm's cabin on Cedar Mountain in the Livermore area.
Leslie, Gladys, Dick, Mabel, Art, and Walter Holm, circa late 1950s

Art Holm's baseball team, Livermore. Art is on the left in the row of kneeling players.

Velma Holm Miller

Verda Holm George

Leslie Holm Sr. with Dorothy "Dodo" Holm Cowell cutting and wrapping meat at the "Little House" on Fair View farm

Art Holm's granddaughter Shirley Miller

Art Holm's twin granddaughters, Sandy and Sharon George, with cousin Linda Miller

Art Holm, daughter Velma, Dick Holm, and Leslie Holm before Leslie was sent to France to serve in World War I. circa 1918

Citrus Spritzer

NANCY CALHOUN MUELLER

Makes 2 quarts

3 (1-inch) strips orange zest
3 (1-inch) strips grapefruit zest
4 cups pineapple-orange juice
2 cups freshly squeezed pink
    grapefruit juice
2 cups chilled sparkling mineral water

Place the citrus zest in a glass pitcher and crush slightly by gently pressing them against the pitcher with the back of a spoon. Add the juices, and stir well. Cover and chill thoroughly. Stir in the sparkling water just before serving. Serve over ice.

Stanley Jorgensen, Dan Fachner, Dick Holm (the teetotaler!) and Carl Stebbins

Lime Sunrise

NANCY CALHOUN MUELLER

Makes 2¼ quarts

2 cups pineapple juice
2 cups cranberry juice cocktail
½ cup freshly squeezed lime juice
1 (11.5-ounce) can apricot nectar
9 slices fresh lime
2 (12-ounce) cans ginger ale

In a large pitcher, combine the fruit juices and lime slices, cover and chill. Add the ginger ale just before serving and stir. Pour over ice.

Good Morning, Merry Sunshine

When we were young, we often spent the night with Papa and Granny. As we were eating our breakfast in the morning, Papa (who had already been outside working for a few hours), would sing us a very animated version of this traditional lullaby, which he learned in school in 1906. He would sing the last verse in a deep comical voice. Today when we are on vacation, I sing this to the last person sleeping, while marching through their bedroom giving them a pan parade.
    — *Nancy Calhoun Mueller*

Good morning merry sunshine,
How did you wake so soon?
You've scared the little stars away,
And shined away the moon.
I saw you go to sleep last night,
Before I ceased my playing,
How did you get way over there,
And where have you been staying?

I never go to sleep, dear child
I just go round to see
My little children of the East,
Who rise and watch for me.
I waken all the little birdies
And flowers on my way,
Then last of all, the little child
Who stayed out late to play.

Blue Balls

Makes 6 shots

A rather potent shot that will sneak up on you! This is a recipe for a six-shooter. For one shot, use a sixth of the ingredients. The intoxicologist (bartender) instruments that you will need are a shaker, a strainer, a jigger, a pint glass, and six shot glasses. Being a Holm, I like to share with the family. Enjoy.

MARIO GARCIA

Enough ice to fill half the shaker
4 ounces pineapple juice
2 ounces Bacardi 151 rum
2 ounces Bacardi light rum
2 ounces coconut rum
1½ ounces blue curaçao

Line up the 6 shot glasses. Fill the shaker half full of ice. Pour in the pineapple juice, 151 rum, light rum, coconut rum, and blue curaçao. Fit the pint glass upside down in the shaker (just like in the movies). Shake until it is nice and blue-green. Remove the pint glass, place a strainer over the shaker, and pour evenly into the shot glasses. Find 6 brave people, and bottoms up. Cheers!

Warren Howe, Dave Holm, Marcos Garcia, and Mario Garcia in the Jack Daniels Saloon at the Livermore Rodeo

Remembering *Ione*

When I was about eleven years old, I was up at Granny's house playing, like always. While running around, I slid and fell on my hands and knees on the driveway. Cut and bleeding, I went into the house. Nurse Granny took me to her bathroom. At the time I didn't realize why David was laughing, but I was soon to find out. Granny opened her medicine cabinet and grabbed a little bottle of **Red Stuff**. I had no idea what was in store for me. All I knew was that Granny was going to make it feel better. Oh, dear God, was I wrong! I guess at my young age I didn't realize that Granny had taken care of hellions such as my Grandpa Frank and David. By the time it came to me, all sympathy was gone. Granny dabbed a little of this **Red Stuff** on a cotton ball and placed it on the open cut on my knee—I think I blacked out. I tried to run, but this lady was unusually strong. Again, I forgot whom she had had to deal with, and I didn't have a chance. I came back into the living room where David was sitting, laughing. I asked him what that **Red Stuff** was. He laughed and said, "Merthiolate." He then told me that Granny had had that bottle since he was a kid. That was the first and last time I asked Granny for a Band-Aid.

~ *Mario Garcia*

Lemon Drop Jell-o Shooters

Makes 12 shooters

It's possible to create many variations of this recipe. I have also made margarita shooters with lime-flavored gelatin, tequila, and Triple Sec, using the same measurements. I omit the sugar for this variation, but you could substitute sa't on the rim, if desired. Try creating your favorite drink in gelatin form—just substitute the alcohol for the cold water when making the gelatin. I prefer to use small plastic cups for shooters as they do not get soggy.
My friends always request that I bring shooters to their parties.

SUSIE CALHOUN

1 (6-ounce) box lemon gelatin mix
2 cups boiling water
1¾ cups lemon-flavored vodka
½ cup Triple Sec, divided
¼ cup sugar
12 (3-ounce) plastic cups

Dissolve the lemon gelatin in the boiling water in a mixing bowl. (For easy pouring, I use a 2-quart Pyrex measuring bowl with a pour spout.) Stir in the lemon vodka and ¼ cup of the Triple Sec. Pour the remaining Triple Sec into a small dish. Pour the sugar into another small, shallow dish. Dip the rim of the cups first in the Triple Sec and then into the sugar to create a sugar rim. Evenly fill the small cups with the gelatin mixture. Chill for approximately 1 hour. Then sprinkle the top of each cup with a pinch of the remaining sugar. Return the cups to the refrigerator and chill until they are completely firm, about another hour. Loosen the edges of each cup with a knife. Shoot it if you dare—but a spoon may come in handy!

Troy Bowers and Susie Calhoun at the Viaggio, Reno

The Calhoun Sisters: Susie Calhoun, Merry Carter, and Nancy Mueller with Irish Coffees at the annual trek to a San Francisco Giants game

The Perfect Cosmopolitan

Makes 1 serving

Be sure to use a chilled martini glass. Caution: one is good, two is great, three is a really bad idea.

STACI HOLM BROWN

1 lemon or lime wedge

Sugar for coating the rim

Crushed ice

4 ounces Absolut Citron vodka or other
 lemon-flavored vodka

2 ounces Triple Sec

2 ounces cranberry juice

Splash of Rose's lime juice (or fresh)

Squeeze of lemon

Lemon or lime twist, for garnish

Wet the rim of a chilled martini glass with the lemon wedge. Dip the rim in sugar to coat. In a stainless-steel shaker full of crushed ice, combine the vodka, Triple Sec, cranberry juice, and citrus juices. Shake. Strain the contents into a martini glass. Serve with a lemon or lime twist.

Wedding of Staci Holm and Peter Brown, 2000
Bob and Deanna Holm, Staci and Peter, and Bryan Holm

Irish Cream

Makes 6 servings

You may need Tums after drinking—these can give heartburn to the unsuspecting.

LOU ANN MCCUNE

1¾ cups Irish whiskey

1 (14-ounce) can sweetened
 condensed milk

1 cup whipping cream

4 eggs

2 tablespoons chocolate syrup

2 teaspoons instant coffee

1 teaspoon vanilla extract

½ teaspoon almond extract

Combine all the ingredients in a blender and blend well. Chill in the refrigerator, then serve.

Tom Mullarkey, Susie Calhoun, Abraham Lincoln, Lou Ann McCune, and Troy Bowers (Susie's husband) at Stevenot Winery, 2005

Iced Coffee

Makes 4 servings

I can never get enough coffee. As far as vices go, if coffee is my worst, I can live with that. When working at Concannon Vineyard, a young Bostonian, Marybeth, shared her mother's iced coffee recipe with me. No more excuses to avoid coffee on a hot afternoon.

NANCY CALHOUN MUELLER

4 cups coffee
Sugar
Milk

Brew a pot of coffee in the morning. Pour into a heatproof pitcher and add sugar to taste. Chill for a few hours. Add your choice of milk to the pitcher. Serve over ice. You can keep some frozen coffee ice cubes in the freezer if you don't want to water down your coffee.

Cowboy Coffee

Makes eight 1-cup servings

During my teens and twenties, I spent a lot of quality time with my grandfather, Dick Holm. Besides thoroughly enjoying Papa's company and learning his cowboy ways, I also enjoyed many cups of his cowboy coffee. To measure the ground coffee, he used one of Granny's Blue Denmark coffee cups, which was missing its handle, and he boiled the coffee in an old, worn coffee pot. I can still smell the coffee as it boiled over on the stove, leaving coffee grounds stuck to the side of the pot and on the stove— which I'm sure Granny just loved cleaning up later. The addition of an eggshell helps keep the grounds on the bottom of the pot.

MERRY "LAMBIE" CALHOUN CARTER

2 quarts water
¾ cup ground coffee
1 eggshell (rinsed)

Bring the water to a boil in a coffee pot. Add the coffee grounds and the eggshell to the boiling water. Return the water to a boil and boil for about 5 minutes. Remove the pot from the heat and let it stand for 2 minutes to allow the grounds to settle. Pour and enjoy.

Back: Stanley Jorgensen, Dick Holm, Louie Draghi, Les Holm Jr., Wayne Calhoun, Frank Holm, Russ Rasmussen, Chet Sandbeck Kneeling in front: Tony George Seated in front: Jim Holm Sr., Dale Andersen

Livermore's chapter of the Dania Society was founded in 1892. This society provided Danish immigrants an opportunity to make friends with those who spoke their native language and could offer assistance and advice on living in this new land. Many Danes, both men and women, enjoyed dancing and playing cards. The two-story Dania Hall was built in 1911 on Second and N streets. Upstairs was a large room for meetings and dancing. The downstairs was used for banquets and social events. Holm family members who were children in the 1930s through the 1960s remember the smell of coffee and hot chocolate and platters of sandwiches, cookies, and cakes at the Dania Christmas Party. Children would eat first; then the adults, who could hear the children playing upstairs. Children would recite poems, sing, or play the piano and other musical instruments. With the singing of "Jingle Bells," Santa would appear, gathering the children into a circle. He presented each with a red net stocking containing an apple, an orange, and hard Christmas candy. This was a real treat. Everyone then danced. As children, we loved the Danish polka, stamping our feet, singing "One, two, three, dah-ta-dah-ta-dah-ta," and then dancing.

— Tilli Calhoun

The Dania Society

Original drawing of Dania Hall by Tilli Calhoun

Mabel Holm and Carl Jorgensen,
February 1914

Phyllis Jorgensen Fachner

Stanley and Phyllis Jorgensen
at Fair View, 1920

Scott Moore,
Steven Miller,
Michelle Miller,
Santa, Wendy
Moore (on floor),
Kristine Diltz,
and Janet Fachner
(Santa's helper)

Easter, 1957, at Coco and Jim Regnolds's
with Mabel Holm Jorgensen's grandchildren.
Back: Gayle Fachner, Vickie Regnolds,
Carol Jorgensen Middle: Janet Fachner,
Lynn Jorgensen, Bill Jorgensen Front: Carl
Jorgensen (with the dog Tar)
Randy Regnolds, Danny Fachner

Coco Jorgensen Regnolds, Stanley
Jorgensen, and Phyllis Jorgensen Fachner

Mabel and Jake Rees

Jim's Meatballs

Makes approximately 50 ¾-inch meatballs

These were the greatest appetizer meatballs on Christmas Eve.

JIM HOLM SR.

1 pound ground beef
¾ teaspoon salt
1 tablespoon chopped onion
½ cup soft bread crumbs
¼ cup milk
1 tablespoon flour, more as needed
2 tablespoons butter, more as needed
3 tablespoons molasses
3 tablespoons prepared mustard
3 tablespoons vinegar
¼ cup ketchup
¼ teaspoon dried thyme

In a bowl, break up the meat with a fork, sprinkle with salt, and add the onion. In a small bowl, mix the bread crumbs and milk, and combine with the meat mixture. Sprinkle the flour on a plate or countertop. Over medium heat, melt a tablespoon of butter in a frying pan. Form the meat into ¾-inch balls, roll in the flour, and sauté in the butter until browned on all sides and cooked through. Remove from the heat.

In a small bowl, combine the molasses, mustard, vinegar, ketchup, and thyme; blend until smooth. Pour the sauce over the meatballs in the frying pan and return to the heat. Simmer, stirring occasionally, until the sauce thickens and the meatballs are glazed, 8 to 10 minutes. Keep hot in a chafing dish.

Jimmy Holm and nephew Gary Holm

Hank and Patsy Neely with Carol and Jim Holm

In the Danish tradition, Carl and Ida Holm would host a family gathering on Christmas Eve. A Christmas tree was set up in the parlor and the house decorated with holly berries. Dinner included a variety of meats, red cabbage, salads, and desserts. After dinner, Santa would make a noisy arrival and distribute gifts. Later, all would join in, singing songs of the 1930s and 1940s.

Dick and Ione Holm continued the Christmas tradition, which evolved into an extended family gathering beginning at noon on Christmas Eve. The family continues to gather at Wendy and Warren Howe's home on Mines Road. A variety of sandwiches, relishes, and desserts are brought for all to share. It is an afternoon of eating and visiting. In the evening Santa still makes a noisy appearance, but only when he hears the singing of "Jingle Bells." There is a flurry of gift opening, with paper everywhere, and another round of dinner. This holiday continues to be a favorite for all, filled with warm family memories.

— Tilli Calhoun

Clam Dip

Makes about 1½ cups

I've brought this to family get-togethers. One minute it's there, the next it's gone!

LORI NEELY SOUTH

1 (6-ounce) can of minced clams
1 (8-ounce) package cream cheese, softened
1 tablespoon mayonnaise
½ teaspoon finely chopped green onion
1 teaspoon lemon juice
½ teaspoon garlic salt
⅛ teaspoon Worcestershire sauce
Dash of Tabasco

Drain the minced clams, reserving some of the clam juice in case it is needed later. In a bowl, combine the cream cheese, mayonnaise, green onion, lemon juice, garlic salt, Worcestershire sauce, and Tabasco. Add the clams and mix thoroughly. If the dip is too thick, add some of the clam juice and stir well. Serve with chips or crackers.

Hot Dip

Makes about 3 cups

The grandkids look forward to this recipe amid the snacks we have before the "spread" of food that is always served whenever you are at Granny's.

JOAN VOERCKEL HOLM

1 (8-ounce) package cream cheese
1 (15-ounce) can Dennison's chili (without beans)
½ cup prepared taco sauce
1 (16-ounce) package corn chips

In a microwave-safe bowl, soften the cream cheese. Add the chili and mix well. Add the taco sauce and blend thoroughly. Microwave for 4 minutes or until hot. Serve with the chips.

Vivian's Garlic Dip

Makes 1 cup

I can't describe how good this is. Serve it with crackers or raw vegetables. It is also good as a sandwich spread. Try to make this 2 to 3 days ahead of time. The longer it sits, the better it gets.

Becky Calhoun Foster

1 (8.5-ounce) jar oil-packed sun dried tomatoes, cut into small pieces (reserve the oil)

3 cloves garlic, minced

1 handful fresh basil leaves, chopped

1 (8-ounce) package cream cheese, softened

½ cup plain yogurt or sour cream

In a small bowl, combine the tomatoes, garlic, basil, and the reserved oil from the sun dried tomatoes, and toss lightly. Let marinate for up to 3 days.

Drain the excess oil from the tomato mixture and discard the oil. Place the tomato mixture in a mixing bowl, add the cream cheese, and blend together. Add enough yogurt to get the desired consistency.

Dill Dip

Makes 2 cups

I was looking through an old recipe collection that contained some of my favorite recipes from the 1970s, and I found dips that made appearances at many family gatherings, and at the parties Gayle Koopman and I had in our duplex on Linden Street in Livermore. Make this dip the day before or at least hours before serving so that the flavors have time to develop.

Merry "Lambie" Calhoun Carter

1 cup sour cream

1 cup mayonnaise

1 teaspoon dried dill weed

1 tablespoon dried parsley

1 tablespoon chopped green onion

Pinch of salt

In a small bowl, mix all the ingredients. Keep in the refrigerator until ready to serve.

Tilli Calhoun, Grand Marshal of the 2007 Livermore Rodeo Parade. Husband Wayne and granddaughters Whitney and Laina Carter are in the car with her.

Hot Stuffed Green Olives

Serves 8

STANLEY AND EDNA JORGENSEN

2 cups shredded sharp Cheddar cheese

½ cup (1 stick) butter or margarine

1 cup flour

½ teaspoon salt

1 teaspoon paprika

60 stuffed green olives, any variety

In a bowl, blend the grated cheese and butter. Sift together the flour, salt, and paprika and add to the cheese mixture. This will make a fairly stiff dough. Pinch off a small amount of dough, flatten it in the palm of your hand, and wrap it around an olive. Freeze the wrapped olives. Do not defrost before baking. When ready to serve, preheat the oven to 400°F and bake for 15 minutes or until golden. Serve hot.

Tostada Dip

Serves 12

ELEANOR BARBERA

1 (16-ounce) can refried beans

1 (7-ounce) can chopped Ortega chilies

3 tablespoons mild taco sauce

2 cups guacamole dip

1 small bell pepper, finely chopped
   (optional)

1 ripe tomato, finely diced

2 stalks of celery, finely chopped
   (optional)

1 pint sour cream

1 small head of lettuce, finely shredded

½ pound sharp Cheddar cheese, shredded

½ pound Monterey Jack cheese, shredded

On a plate or shallow bowl, spread the refried beans. In this order, add layers of chilies, taco sauce, and guacamole dip. In a small bowl, combine the bell pepper, tomato, and celery. Spread on top of the layers. Next, add a layer of sour cream on top of the chopped vegetables. Top with the lettuce, then the cheeses, and serve.

Cleaning the pool at the Circle H Ranch: Supervisor Dick Holm, Tina Stebbins Barbera, Wayne Calhoun, Craig Teel, Joe Barbera

Nuts and Bolts

Serves 12

Be sure to use high-quality nuts. When we make this recipe, we like to use extra-large cashews.

SUSIE CALHOUN *from Granny's friend, Minnie Lyons*

½ cup vegetable oil

¾ cup (1½ sticks) margarine, melted

5 tablespoons Worcestershire sauce

1 tablespoon garlic powder

1 tablespoon celery salt

½ tablespoon Lawry's Seasoning Salt

1 envelope Lipton Onion Soup Mix

1 (12-ounce) package Crispix or
     Wheat Chex

1 (12-ounce) package pretzel sticks

1½ to 2 pounds mixed nuts

Preheat the oven to 225°F. In a blender, mix the oil, margarine, Worcestershire sauce, garlic powder, celery salt, Lawry's, and soup mix. Combine the Crispix, pretzels, and nuts in an 8-quart bowl or roasting pan. Add the oil-seasoning mixture and toss gently. Spread on several jelly roll pans and bake at least 2 hours or until lightly browned and crispy. Stir frequently. Spread on paper towels and cool overnight. Store in air-tight containers.

Granny's Deviled Eggs

Makes 12 appetizers

IONE TEETER HOLM

6 hard-cooked eggs, cooled and peeled

¼ cup mayonnaise

1 tablespoon ketchup

1 tablespoon mustard

1 teaspoon Worcestershire sauce

Salt and pepper

Chopped fresh chives, minced fresh
     parsley, or paprika, for garnish

Slice the hard-cooked eggs in half lengthwise. Scoop out the yolks, mash with a fork, and combine with the mayonnaise, ketchup, mustard, and Worcestershire until creamy. Season to taste with salt and pepper. Fill the hollow of each egg white with the yolk mixture. Garnish with chives, parsley, or paprika.

This saying, sewn as a sampler, hung in Granny's kitchen

No Matter Where I Serve My Guests It Seems They Like My Kitchen Best

Betty Cleveland's Cheese Balls

Makes about 2 cups (2 cheese balls)

Betty Cleveland was president of our school employees union in Livermore when I was a member. She served these appetizers at a union function. Betty's sons, Rick and Rex, had a band that played at the wedding of my sister Nancy and her husband, Bob. It was held at Dania Hall.

SUSIE CALHOUN

2 (8-ounce) packages of cream cheese,
    at room temperature
½ cup chopped red and green bell peppers
1 (8-ounce) can crushed pineapple,
    drained
½ cup chopped, toasted pecans

In a medium-size bowl, thoroughly combine the cream cheese, peppers, and pineapple. Chill in the refrigerator until the mixture begins to firm up, about 30 minutes. Using a spatula, divide the mixture in half and form each portion into a ball. Spread the pecans in a shallow dish, place a cheese ball on the nuts, and roll around to coat completely. Repeat with the second ball. Serve with crackers.

Papa, Granny, newlyweds Nancy and Bob Mueller, Tilli and Wayne Calhoun

Artichoke Frittata

Serves 8

If you would like thinner squares, use a larger pan.

LORI NEELY SOUTH

2 (6.5-ounce) jars marinated artichoke
    hearts, chopped, reserve oil from 1 jar
1 bunch green onions, chopped
4 eggs
6 soda crackers, crumbled
1 clove garlic, minced
Dash of Tabasco sauce
Salt and pepper
¼ cup fresh parsley, finely chopped
½ pound sharp Cheddar cheese, shredded
    (about 2 cups)

Preheat the oven to 325°F. Use a small amount of the reserved oil to season an 8- by 8-inch ovenproof pan. Pour the remainder of the oil into a frying pan over medium heat. Add the green onions and sauté until transparent; do not brown. Drain the green onions on a paper towel. In a bowl, beat the eggs. Add the cracker crumbs, garlic, and Tabasco. Season with salt and pepper to taste and combine well. Add the green onions, artichoke hearts, parsley, and cheese and mix well. Pour into the pan and bake until just set in the middle, about 35 minutes. To serve, cool slightly and cut into squares.

Zucchini Frittata

Serves 8

BOBBIE LIVERMORE BAIRD

½ cup salad oil plus more to oil the baking dish
4 eggs, beaten
Handful fresh parsley, chopped
½ teaspoon dried marjoram
1 clove garlic, minced
Salt and pepper
1 cup Bisquick baking mix
3 cups thinly-sliced zucchini
½ onion, chopped
½ cup grated Parmesan cheese

Preheat the oven to 350°F. Oil a 9- by 12-inch baking dish. In a bowl, whisk together the eggs and oil. Mix in the parsley, marjoram, and garlic. Season with salt and pepper to taste. Add the Bisquick and mix well. Fold in the zucchini, onion, and cheese. Bake for approximately 25 minutes or until the eggs are set and the top is slightly browned.

Robert Livermore

In 1869, William Mendenhall established a 100 acre townsite on his property. He named it for his friend and fellow rancher, Robert Livermore, who had held the second largest land grant in the area. Livermore died in 1858 before the establishment of the town that would bear his name. Mendenhall donated lands for a school, railroad depot, college, and cemetery. Bobbie Livermore Baird is Robert's great-great-granddaughter.

Bobbie Baird's parents, Bob and Nada Livermore at the Livermore family ranch on Mines Road.

William Mendenhall

Photos courtesy of the Livermore Heritage Guild

Crab Fu Yung

Everyone loved to come when Jim served his Chinese dinners at parties for friends. This was one of his recipes—so good!

CAROL HOLM NEWMAN

Cakes

1 cup bean sprouts

1 cup crabmeat

3 tablespoons oil

½ cup coarsely grated onion

½ cup diced celery

6 eggs

1 tablespoon soy sauce

1 tablespoon cornstarch

1 teaspoon salt

Dash pepper

Sauce

½ cup water

2 teaspoons cornstarch

2 teaspoons sherry

1 tablespoon soy sauce

Preheat the oven to low to keep the cakes warm as you cook them.

If you are using canned sprouts, drain off the liquid. Combine the crabmeat and bean sprouts in a bowl. In a frying pan over medium heat, add 1 tablespoon of the oil and sauté the onion and celery until soft; add to the crabmeat mixture. In a bowl, beat the eggs. Whisk in the soy sauce, cornstarch, salt, and pepper. Fold in the crabmeat and vegetables and mix well. Using the same pan over medium heat, add another tablespoon of the oil. When the oil is hot, add tablespoon-size portions of the crab and egg mixture to the pan. Brown one side, turn, and brown the other side. Keep the cakes warm on a large heat-resistant platter in the oven until all are cooked.

While you are frying the cakes, prepare the sauce as follows. In a small pot, whisk together the water and cornstarch. Over medium-high heat, add the sherry and soy sauce. Cook until the liquid thickens enough to coat the back of a spoon, stirring occasionally.

To serve, remove the platter of cakes from the oven, pour the sauce over the cakes, and serve immediately.

Jim Holm Jr. carrying on the tradition of carving the Christmas Eve ham.

Jim Holm Sr. carving the Sunday roast. When the family dogs smelled the irresistible aroma of Granny's Sunday roast, they would run into the kitchen and wait patiently for any small tidbit.

Crab Dip in Red Cabbage

Serves 12

To vary this dip, you can substitute shrimp or clams for the crabmeat. I serve Wheat Thins alongside for dipping.

SUSIE CALHOUN

1 medium-sized head red cabbage
1 red onion, finely diced
2 (6-ounce) cans crabmeat
8 ounces softened cream cheese
1 cup mayonnaise
1 tablespoon Worcestershire sauce
1 teaspoon prepared horseradish

Cut a thin slice from the bottom of the cabbage so it sits flat, then carefully hollow out the inside, saving the cabbage that you remove. Chop or shred enough of this cabbage to yield 1½ cups. Save the rest for another use. In a bowl, combine the cabbage, onion, and crabmeat. In another small bowl, blend together the cream cheese and mayonnaise. Add the Worcestershire sauce and horseradish and continue to mix. Pour this dressing over the cabbage mixture, gently tossing to mix well. Spoon into the hollowed-out cabbage and serve.

Shrimp Spread

Serves 12

I serve this spread with crackers such as Wheat Thins or Triscuits. It may be made one or two days ahead of time.

SANDY SPORTS HOLM

1 envelope Knox unflavored gelatin
3 tablespoons water
1 can Campbell's shrimp soup
1 (6-ounce) can shrimp, drained
½ cup finely chopped yellow onion
1 cup finely chopped celery
1 cup mayonnaise
Leafy greens for serving

In a small bowl, dissolve the gelatin in the water. In a pot, combine the gelatin-water mixture with the soup. Bring the mixture to a boil. Remove from the heat and add the shrimp, onion, celery, and mayonnaise. Combine thoroughly. Pour into a 1-quart mold or serving bowl and chill until firm. To serve, invert the mold on a platter covered with a bed of greens.

Cowboy Caviar

Serves 12

This is a staple at Tilli and Wayne Calhoun's parties at their Party Barn. You can substitute pinto or black beans for the black-eyed peas called for in the recipe.

NANCY CALHOUN MUELLER

2 tablespoons white vinegar
1½ teaspoons olive oil
3 cloves garlic, minced
1 jalapeño pepper, seeds removed and minced
2 firm, ripe avocados, cut into ½-inch dice
1 (15-ounce) can black-eyed peas, drained and rinsed
1 (14-ounce) package frozen corn kernels, thawed
1 red onion, finely chopped
⅔ cup chopped fresh cilantro
4 to 6 tomatoes, coarsely chopped
Salt and pepper
1 (6-ounce) bag tortilla chips

In a large bowl, whisk together the vinegar, oil, garlic, and pepper. Add the avocado to the vinegar mixture and gently toss. Add the peas, corn, onion, cilantro, and tomatoes to the avocado mixture; mix gently. Season with salt and pepper to taste. Spoon into a dish and serve with the tortilla chips.

Branding at the Circle H Ranch on Mines Road: Don Rasmussen, Ken Calhoun, Aaron Rasmussen, Leslie Holm Sr., Tony George, Rich Holm, Jim Holm Sr., Wayne Calhoun, Dick Holm, Stanley Jorgensen, and Fred Shepherd

Honey Chicken Wings

I have had this recipe for years. I like to make a huge batch and eat them for lunch or dinner. They are also good cold. For a more exotic flavor, you can replace the vegetable oil with sesame oil and sprinkle the chicken with sesame seeds during the last 10 minutes of cooking.

BECKY CALHOUN FOSTER

24 chicken wings or drumettes
　(about 3 pounds)
1 cup honey
½ cup ketchup
½ cup soy sauce
2 teaspoons vegetable oil
2 large cloves of garlic, crushed
　and minced
Pepper (optional)

Preheat the oven to 375°F. Cut off the bony wings tips and discard. Cut each wing in half at the joint. Place them in a single layer in a shallow 3-quart baking dish.

In a medium bowl, combine the honey, ketchup, soy sauce, oil, garlic, and pepper and mix until well blended. Pour the sauce over the chicken pieces, turning them to coat.

Bake for 1¼ to 1½ hours or until browned, occasionally basting them with the juices and sauce from the bottom of the pan. To serve, transfer to a chafing dish or serve hot from the oven.

Bruschetta

Serves 12

Fettunta is toast rubbed with garlic and drenched in olive oil and sea salt. It is called bruschetta when it is topped with a mixture of tomatoes and basil.

MERILYN "TILLI" HOLM CALHOUN

One sourdough baguette, cut into
　⅜-inch slices
2 tablespoons olive oil
¼ cup shredded mozzarella cheese
3 diced tomatoes
1 tablespoon chopped fresh basil
Salt and pepper

Preheat the oven to 400°F. Brush olive oil on both sides of the bread slices. Place them on a cookie sheet and bake until lightly golden, not hard toasted, 3 to 5 minutes. Sprinkle the toasts with the cheese. In a small bowl, toss together the tomatoes and basil; season with salt and pepper to taste. Place a spoonful on each toast and serve.

Try another version–

Rub the baguette toasts with a garlic clove, top with tomato, capers, mozzarella cheese, pine nuts, and black olives. Bake in a preheated 400°F oven for 3 to 5 minutes or until the cheese is bubbling.

Mountain Oysters

First you need a rancher to provide the required ingredient (calf testicles). After any roundup, you find yourself with a bucketful, and they are too good to waste.

BOBBIE LIVERMORE BAIRD

To prepare for cooking, clean the testicles in cold water, then peel off the outer layer of skin. To blanch, cover them with cold water mixed with the juice of 1 lemon. Bring slowly to a boil and simmer, uncovered, for 2 to 5 minutes. Drain and plunge quickly into a pot of cold water. Let cool and drain again. Remove any tubes or membrane. Chill before cutting into desired size (probably in half or slices). You may then use them in sweetbread recipes, substituting them for the sweetbreads. Or, try this simple recipe with sliced testicles.

Dust the testicles lightly with flour. In a frying pan over medium heat, add a couple tablespoons of olive oil. Add a few sliced garlic cloves and sauté until golden. Add the testicles and sauté until browned, 2 to 3 minutes each side. Add ½ cup or so white wine and season to taste with salt and pepper. Cover and cook gently until tender, about 10 minutes. Serve immediately.

Harvesting the "oysters" at the Circle H Ranch

Marinated Mushrooms

Serves 24

You can save and reuse this marinade or use it as a dressing.

FRANK HOLM

5 cloves garlic
⅓ cup olive oil
⅔ cup white wine vinegar
⅓ cup dry red wine
2 tablespoons soy sauce
2 tablespoons honey
2 tablespoons chopped fresh parsley
1 tablespoon salt
2 pounds fresh mushrooms

In a pan over medium heat, sauté the garlic in the oil. Add the vinegar, wine, soy sauce, honey, parsley, and salt. Stir until blended and hot. Put the honey mixture in a large container with a lid. Add the mushrooms and stir to coat the mushrooms. Marinate at least 3 hours, preferably overnight. Stir occasionally.

Cranberry Sauce for Meatballs

Makes about 2½ cups

Tom Neely Family: Tom, Hank, Don, Gene, and Elizabeth, 1943

We like to entertain during the Christmas holiday season, and this has become one of our favorites to serve. Guests always ask for the recipe. I sometimes cheat and use the frozen pre-cooked meatballs from Sam's Club.

DEL SHULT NEELY

1 tablespoon cornstarch
1 tablespoon hot water
1 (16-ounce) can whole cranberry sauce
⅓ cup firmly packed brown sugar
1 tablespoon lime juice
4 dozen prepared meatballs

Combine the cornstarch and water in a small bowl; stir until smooth. In a large skillet, combine the cranberry sauce, sugar, and lime juice. Cook over medium heat, stirring until the sugar dissolves. Add the cornstarch mixture and cook, stirring constantly, until the sauce thickens. Stir in the meatballs. Transfer to a 2-quart casserole, cover, and refrigerate for 8 hours or overnight to allow flavors to blend.

When ready to serve, remove from the refrigerator. Preheat the oven to 350°F. Cover the dish and bake 30 to 35 minutes or until the meatballs are warmed through. Serve warm.

The Neely brothers: Gene, Don, and Hank with their father, Tom

Hank, Don, and Gene Neely with their mother, Elizabeth

Caponatina Sicilian à la Vanna

Serves 8

I find that a large electric skillet is convenient for preparing this recipe. I usually bring a bowl of this to the parties at Tilli and Wayne Calhoun's barn.

VANNA BORN

¼ cup plus 2 tablespoons olive oil
1 large unpeeled eggplant, cut into 1-inch cubes
1 large onion, sliced
2 large celery stalks, thinly sliced
½ (8-ounce) can tomato sauce, thinned with 1 tablespoon water
¼ cup sliced green olives
2 tablespoons pine nuts, toasted
2 tablespoons capers
Salt and pepper
2 tablespoons sugar
3 tablespoons red wine vinegar

Heat ¼ cup of the oil in a large skillet over medium heat. Add the eggplant and sauté until lightly browned, stirring frequently. Cover, reduce the heat to low, and steam for about 10 minutes, or until soft. Stir frequently to keep the eggplant cubes from sticking to the bottom of the skillet.

Remove the eggplant from the pan and place it in a bowl. Add the 2 tablespoons of oil to the pan, then the onion and sauté until golden brown. Add the celery and tomato sauce and simmer for about 15 minutes, or until the celery is softened. Return the eggplant to the skillet and add the olives, pine nuts, and capers. Season with salt and pepper to taste.

In a small bowl, dissolve the sugar in the vinegar. Add to the eggplant mixture, stirring to distribute the flavors. Simmer for about 30 minutes. Stir occasionally, adding water as needed to keep the mixture from drying out. Adjust the vinegar and sugar to taste. Serve with crackers.

Susie Calhoun, Wendy Neely Howe, and Vanna Born at the Party Barn on New Year's Day, 2002

Chips and Queso Texas Style

Makes about 3 cups

I use a slow cooker to make this dip, but a regular pot over medium-low heat would work, too. I've even used the microwave when in a real hurry. Here in Texas, RoTel is the preferred brand of salsa. I use the mild RoTel Original diced tomatoes and green chiles, but you can use whatever brand you prefer.

JAMIE SOUTH

1 (16-ounce) package Velveeta cheese,
    cut into 1-inch squares
1 (10-ounce) can salsa
1 (12-ounce) bag tortilla chips

Set the slow cooker temperature to medium. When it reaches the correct temperature, add the cheese. Stir occasionally as it melts, approximately 10 minutes. Reduce the heat in the slow cooker to warm. Stir in the salsa and let simmer for 10 minutes. To serve, transfer the cheese dip to a bowl. Serve with the tortilla chips.

Rattlesnake à la Mines Road

Number of servings depends on the size of the snake

Available in the summertime only. City folks can eat these appetizers by skewering them with a toothpick. Country folks eat them with their fingers as they are full of bones and easier to eat this way.

BOBBIE LIVERMORE BAIRD

1 fresh-killed rattlesnake,
    3 to 4 feet in length
2 to 3 tablespoons melted butter
    or olive oil
2 cloves garlic, minced
Dash dried oregano
Salt and pepper
½ cup white wine

Remove the snake head and rattles. You can save the rattles, but dispose of the head safely. (We used to bury it.) Slit the underside of the body with a sharp knife and peel back the skin–it will come off like panty hose. Tack the skin to a board to dry, and cover it with salt or borax. The innards will fall out neatly. Trim around the butt and remove the internal organs. Rinse the snake and pat dry, inside and out. Cut the snake into 2- to 3-inch lengths.

In a large skillet over medium heat, add the melted butter. Add the snake and cook it until browned. Add the garlic, oregano, and season with salt and pepper to taste. Add the wine, then cover the pan and simmer until tender, approximately 30 minutes.

Original painting by Tilli Calhoun

Rodeo!

The Livermore Rodeo has always been an important event for the Holm family. The first rodeo in 1918 was held to support the Red Cross. Grandma Ida Holm, known to be a good cook, was asked by the rodeo directors to make lunch for the crowd. Throughout the generations, our family involvement included serving as rodeo queens and members of the Stockmen's Association, participating in the rodeo parade, riding bulls, manning the beer booth, making and serving food, and riding in the Grand Entry as well being enthusiastic spectators. Dick Holm ("Papa"), would load up the grandchildren and take them to the Livermore Rodeo, the Salinas Rodeo, the Hayward Rodeo, and a favorite—the Grand National Rodeo at the Cow Palace in San Francisco.

Cover of the June 2002 Livermore Rodeo program (Original painted by Tilli Calhoun)

Rodeo Grand Entry, 1949
Right to left: Circle H Ranch riders Leslie and Lois Holm, Frank and Joan Holm, Aaron and Sylvia Rasmussen, Wayne and Tilli Calhoun, and Patsy Holm

Rodeo gals Susie and Merry Calhoun, 1959

At the rodeo parade
Back: Carla Stebbins, Evelyn Hansen Beebe, Tilli Calhoun, Mabel Rees.
Front: Gladys Benthien, Grace Gardella, Ben Benthien, Dick Holm, and Ione Holm

Bertha Holm Brown and Billy Brown,
1917

Jams, Jellies,
Pickles, and
Condiments

Mabel and Bertha Holm

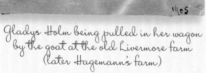

Gladys Holm being pulled in her wagon
by the goat at the old Livermore farm
(later Hagemann's farm)

Back row: Annie Tretzel Holm,
Walter, Mabel, Art, Ida, and Carl
Holm. Front row: Gladys, Bertha
and Dick Holm at the old Livermore
farm, 1905

Back: Mabel Holm with her
Rasmussen cousin, Arthur and
Bertha Holm. Middle: Ida
Holm (seated), Dick and Gladys
Holm on swing. Front: Leslie
Holm, circa 1905

The Holm family on the lawn in front
of the old Livermore farmhouse

Some Basic Canning Information

⌐When canning fruits and vegetables, you need to process them at a high enough temperature for a long enough period of time to destroy the organisms that cause spoilage. You can use a boiling water bath or a steam pressure canner to do this. The following information applies to canning in glass canning jars with lids and screw-on metal bands processed in a water bath canner. This is the process used in this cookbook's canning recipes. If you have a pressure canner, food preparation is the same, but follow the manufacturer's instructions for processing. Fruits, tomatoes, and pickled vegetables can be safely processed using a boiling water bath. However, to process low-acid foods, such as all common vegetables except tomatoes, a steam pressure canner is recommended. For safety, these foods require a temperature higher than boiling water to process in a reasonable amount of time.

⌐Before you begin, make sure all your equipment is clean and working properly. Any large metal container can be used as a water bath canner, provided it is deep enough so that the jars can be covered with two to four inches of briskly boiling water and a rack to hold the jars will fit inside.

⌐Wash glass jars, lids, and bands in hot, soapy water and rinse well. If you are going to hot-pack your fruits or vegetables (see below), sterilize the jars by covering them with water and boiling them for twenty minutes. Metal lids with sealing compound may need to be placed in very hot water for a few minutes; follow the manufacturer's recommendations. Bands can be reused, but lids must be new.

⌐For best results, choose perfect fresh, firm fruits and young, tender vegetables. Sort them for size and ripeness—they'll cook more evenly. Wash them thoroughly, rinsing them a couple times in fresh water. Handle gently to avoid bruising.

⌐Fruits and vegetables may be packed raw or preheated and packed hot. Processing times will vary depending on the method you use. Most raw fruits and vegetables should be packed tightly into the container because they shrink during processing. A few, like corn, lima beans, and peas, should be packed loosely because they expand. Hot foods that are at or near boiling when packed should be packed fairly loosely. There should be enough syrup, water, brine, or juice to fill in around the solid food and cover it. Generally, some space should be left between the packed food and the lid, usually about half an inch.

Kitchen window at the Circle H cabin looking out at the hollyhocks (Original painting by Tilli Calhoun)

⌐To close the jars, wipe the rims clean with a clean cloth, put the lids on—sealing compound down—and screw the metal bands down fairly tight by hand. Put the filled glass jars into a canner filled with hot water. Add boiling water, if needed, to cover the tops of the jars by an inch or two. Don't pour the hot water directly on the jars. Cover the canner. When the water in the canner comes to a rolling boil, start counting the processing time, keeping the water gently boiling. If needed, add more boiling water to keep the jars well covered.

⌐Remove the jars from the canner and place them on a rack or cloth with some space between the jars. Don't set them on a cold surface. After the jars have cooled, check the seals by pressing the middle of the lid with your finger. If the lid springs up when released, the lid is not sealed. Jars that have not sealed properly must be refrigerated and used within three weeks, or change the lid and reprocess. Remove the screw bands and wipe the jars clean. Store in a cool, dry place. Canned foods are best eaten within a year's time.

Amelia's Dills

Makes 6 to 8 quarts

In midsummer, Granny, Papa and I would visit Hagemann Farms, on Stanley Boulevard (where Papa was born), to pick pickling cucumbers. Sometimes we'd buy them already picked. We would can jars and jars of these pickles. Funny thing is, I can't stand dill pickles! The recipe originally came from Amelia Rasmussen. Granny made lots of pickled foods because Papa was so fond of them.

NANCY CALHOUN MUELLER, *with help from Ione Teeter Holm*

6 to 8 quart canning jars, rings, and lids

About 50 pickling cucumbers
1 large bunch fresh dill weed
12 to 16 cloves garlic
1 cup noniodized or pickling salt
1 quart distilled white vinegar
3 quarts water

Prepare the canning jars and lids as described on page 67.

Pack each sterilized jar with 6 to 8 small fresh cucumbers, a sprig of fresh dill, and 1 or 2 cloves garlic. In a nonreactive pot over high heat, combine the salt, vinegar, and water and bring to a rolling boil. Fill each of the packed jars up to ½ inch from the top with the hot pickling liquid and seal. Put the jars in a hot-water bath, cover, bring to a boil, and process for 15 minutes (see page 67). Remove the jars and allow them to cool. Make sure all the lids have sealed. Store for 6 to 8 weeks in a cool, dark place before serving.

Bread and Butter Pickles

Makes 8 to 10 pints

IONE TEETER HOLM

8 to 10 pint canning jars, rings, and lids

25 small cucumbers
8 medium yellow onions
1 quart distilled white vinegar
2 cups sugar
½ cup noniodized salt
2 teaspoons whole celery seed
2 teaspoons ground turmeric
1 teaspoon dry mustard

Wash and slice the cucumbers and onions into ⅛-inch rounds. Soak them overnight in cold water.

When you are ready to proceed, prepare the jars and lids as described on page 67.

Drain the water from the onions and cucumbers. In a nonreactive pot, combine the vinegar, sugar, salt, celery seed, turmeric, and mustard and bring to a boil. Put the cucumbers and onions in a large nonreactive pot, pour the hot liquid over the cucumbers and onions, and let stand for 2 hours. Then, bring the liquid to a boil and boil for 3 minutes. Pack the pickles and liquid in hot jars, leaving ½ inch of space at the top. Seal. Put the jars of pickles in a hot-water bath, cover, bring to a boil, and process for 10 minutes (see page 67). Remove the jars and allow them to cool. Make sure all the lids have sealed. Store in a cool, dark place for 6 to 8 weeks before serving.

Asier (Danish Cucumber Pickles)

Makes 8 pints

From Ione's diary on September 13, 1967: Hot. Dick to Circle H then cut lawn. Patsy & I did 22 pts D. pickles & I did 1 big & 5 small jars peppers. We to Onstad's with Vandales.

IONE TEETER HOLM

8 pint canning jars, rings, and lids

4 very large cucumbers, 10 to 12 inches long
2 to 3 tablespoons noniodized salt
2 cups distilled white vinegar
16 sprigs fresh dill weed

Pickling syrup (makes 1½ quarts)
3 cups distilled white vinegar
3 cups sugar
2 teaspoons pickling spice

Peel the cucumbers, cut in half lengthwise, and scoop out the seeds. Place the cukes in a nonreactive pot, salt heavily, and let them sit overnight. When you are ready to continue, wipe the cukes dry and cut into 1-inch slices. In a nonreactive pot, bring the vinegar to a boil. Slowly pour the boiling vinegar over the cucumbers. Let sit for 15 to 20 minutes.

Prepare the canning jars and lids as described on page 67.

To make the pickling syrup, combine the vinegar, sugar, and pickling spices in a large, nonreactive pot and bring to a boil. Place the cucumbers in the boiling syrup. As soon as the boiling resumes, remove the cucumbers. Place a couple sprigs of fresh dill in each jar, fill the jars halfway with syrup, and pack the jars with the cucumbers. Top off each jar with the remaining syrup, leaving ½ inch of space at the top. Seal the jars with the lids. Place the jars in a hot-water bath, cover, bring to a boil, and process for 5 minutes (see page 67). Remove the jars and allow them to cool. Make sure all the lids have sealed. Store for 6 to 8 weeks in a cool, dark place before serving.

Original painting of Ione's Danish pickles by Tilli Calhoun

Pickled Peppers

Makes 10 quarts

Papa's garden was a wonder of wonders; he could grow anything, and Granny would cook everything. This is her recipe. I remember pickled peppers being a favorite of my uncles Frank, Jimmy, and Richie. They would eat 'em and sweat—very exciting stuff for a kid.

NANCY CALHOUN MUELLER

10 quart canning jars, rings, and lids

8 pounds Hungarian, banana, or
  waxed peppers, washed
3 quarts distilled white vinegar
1 quart water
¼ cup noniodized salt
2 to 3 heads garlic, cloves separated
  and peeeled

Prepare the canning jars and lids as described on page 67.

Make a slit in the side of each pepper; be sure to wear rubber gloves if handling spicy peppers.

Make a canning syrup by combining the vinegar, water, salt, and sugar in a large pot over high heat. Bring to a boil. Meanwhile, tightly pack the hot jars with the whole peppers and 4 to 6 cloves garlic. When the syrup has reached a boil, fill each jar with the liquid, leaving ½ inch of space at the top. Seal and process in a water bath for 10 minutes (see page 67). Remove the jars and allow them to cool. Make sure all the lids have sealed. Store for 6 to 8 weeks in a cool, dark place before serving.

Spiced Pickled Peaches

Makes 24 servings

My mother, Phyllis Jorgensen Fachner, prepares this side dish for family gatherings. My cousin, Vickie Regnolds Warden, still squeals when she sees them on Christmas Eve.

JANET FACHNER VON TOUSSAINT

3 (28-ounce) cans cling peach halves
2 tablespoons distilled white vinegar
2 or 3 cinnamon sticks
Approximately 20 whole cloves

Drain the peach juice into a sauce pan, add the vinegar, cinnamon, and cloves. Bring the juice mixture to a boil and simmer for 5 minutes. Add the peaches and refrigerate in the juice for 2 to 3 days. Drain off the pickling liquid before serving.

*Otto and Phyllis Fachner,
Edna and Stanley Jorgensen,
Coco and Jim Regnolds*

Pickled Olives

Makes 24 quarts

When Don and I were first married, 50 some-odd years ago, Don's mom, Edith Rasmussen, taught me how to cook, including canning. Poor Don—I couldn't even boil an egg. I remember Grandpa Aaron's olive trees all around his house on North Livermore Avenue and how he used to pick olives to give away. I used a huge stoneware crock to hold the olives and brine, but Grandpa Aaron used half a wine barrel. You can buy household lye in the cleaning section of your grocery store. Be careful with it—wear rubber gloves to protect your hands. Keep lemon juice or vinegar handy to neutralize any lye that splashes on your skin.

JANE RASMUSSEN *passed along from Grandpa Aaron Rasmussen*

24 quart canning jars, rings, and lids

6 gallons green olives
2 pounds concentrated lye
12 to 14 pounds noniodized salt

To process the olives, dissolve 1 pound of lye and 4 pounds of salt in 6 gallons of water in a very large crock. Add the olives and soak for 2 days. Stir the olives and brine once a day in order to keep the olives from spotting. A clean broomstick is good for this process. Drain off the brine and rinse the olives in clean water. Dissolve another pound of lye and 4 pounds of salt in 6 gallons of fresh water, add the olives and soak for 2 more days. Stir with the broomstick daily. Drain off the brine again and rinse the olives in clean water. Add 6 more gallons of fresh water and let the olives soak for 5 to 8 more days–until they no longer have a bitter taste. Drain. Make a brine with 3 pounds salt and 4½ gallons fresh water (enough to cover the olives), let the olives soak for 3 days.

Now they are ready to bottle up. Make a fresh batch of brine using the same proportions (3 pounds of salt to 4½ gallons water); bring to a boil. Loosely pack the olives in quart jars. Fill the jars with the fresh hot brine up to ½ inch from the top of the jar and screw on the lids. Invert the jars until cool. Store in a cool, dark place. Olives can be eaten 5 weeks after bottling. The olives will continue to develop a rich flavor the longer they sit. If the olives are too salty for your taste, soak them for a couple hours or overnight in fresh water before eating. Drain and serve. Refrigerate any leftover drained olives and use within 3 days.

Richie Holm, Jane Volponi, Rich Palmer, Frank Holm, and Jane and Don Rasmussen at the Circle H Ranch Annual Deer Barbecue.

Former Superintendent of Schools Joe Michell and Wayne Calhoun at the Annual Deer Barbecue at the Circle H Ranch.

Pickled Beets and Eggs

Serves 8

IONE TEETER HOLM

2 (1-pound) cans whole beets, drained,
    1 cup beet juice reserved
1 small onion, halved and thinly
    sliced into half moons (optional)
8 hard-cooked eggs, peeled
1 cup sugar
¾ cup apple cider vinegar
1½ teaspoons salt
Dash of pepper

Place the beets, onion, and peeled eggs in a glass or plastic container. Set aside.

In a medium-size saucepan, combine the beet juice, sugar, vinegar, salt, and pepper. Bring to a boil, lower the heat, and simmer for 5 minutes. Immediately pour the simmering liquid and spices over the beets and eggs. Cool to room temperature, cover, and refrigerate for 48 hours before serving.

Chow-Chow

Makes 16 pints

This is a recipe of Granny's made with after-harvest vegetables. She used a meat grinder to cut up the vegetables, but today, we use a food processor. Just whirl around everything but the cabbage until it is chopped fairly well. The cabbage we chop very finely with a knife.

IONE TEETER HOLM

16 pint canning jars, rings, and lids

1 peck green tomatoes (8 quarts), ground
1 cup salt
1 medium cabbage
6 green bell peppers
5 red bell peppers
6 medium white onions
3 quarts white distilled vinegar
8 cups sugar
2 tablespoons celery seed
2 tablespoons dry mustard
1 tablespoon ground cloves

In a very large bowl, combine the ground tomatoes and salt. Place in a colander and let drain overnight.

On the following day, grind the cabbage, peppers, and onions. In a large nonreactive pot, combine the vinegar, sugar, celery seed, mustard, and cloves and bring to a boil. Add the tomatoes and other ground ingredients, mix thoroughly. Decrease the heat and cook until tender, about 1 hour. Stir frequently.

While the vegetable mixture is cooking, sterilize 16 pint jars (or 8 quart jars) and lids as described on page 67. Spoon the hot mixture into the hot, sterilized jars, wipe the jar rims with a damp cloth, screw on the lids, and process in a boiling water bath for 10 minutes. Remove the jars and allow them to cool. Make sure all the lids have sealed. Store for 6 to 8 weeks in a cool, dark place before serving.

Zesty Mustard Spread

Makes 3¼ cups

This spread is hot and tangy!

JANE RASMUSSEN *from a recipe that originated with Cranie Walker*

1 (4-ounce) can Colman's dry mustard
1 cup distilled white vinegar
2 eggs, beaten
½ cup sugar
Dash salt
1½ cups mayonnaise

In a nonreactive bowl, combine the mustard and vinegar and let stand overnight.

The following day, in a pot over medium heat, combine the eggs, sugar, salt, and the mustard-vinegar mixture. Cook until it thickens, about 5 minutes, stirring constantly. Allow to cool. Stir in the mayonnaise and mix well. Store in a covered container in the refrigerator.

Circle H Ranch
Standing: John Kiely, Steve Sanders, Bill Jorgensen, Stanley Jorgensen, Bobby Frick, Jim Holm Sr., Chet Sandbeck, Frank Holm, Denny Kiely
Kneeling: Bob Holm, Wayne Calhoun, Dick Holm, Louie Draghi, Tony George

Tommy, Bobby, Carla, and baby Gary

A Memory of Rescue

My Granny and Dede (Gladys and Ben Benthien) lived on the same parcel of land as Dick and Ione. As a child, I was always going back and forth, playing between the two houses. My playmates were those mischievous cousins of mine, Tommy and Bobby Holm. We were everywhere—in the barns, in the pigpen, in the chicken coop, in the horse corral, in the trees, and in the vegetable gardens. Uncle Dick and my Dede always had the most wonderful vegetable gardens. I grew up eating the tastiest corn and the best onions, along with the most delicious artichokes, chard, rhubarb and carrots. One day—it may have been the same day Tommy and Bobby made me slide down the barn roof into the horse corral—we had been checking out Uncle Dick's vegetable garden, when the boys were called home, leaving me on top of the wire fence. I was stuck! Try as I might, I couldn't manage to climb down. With one leg on each side, I was just barely balancing on the top wire. I started screaming, knowing that Granny Holm or my own Granny might hear me. I needed to be rescued. After what seemed like some very, very long, frustrating minutes, as any seven- or eight-year-old would do, I started crying. Finally, after more screaming, my Granny heard my cries and at last rescued me from atop that fence.

— Carla Stebbins Canter

Quince Jelly

When I married Bill Jorgensen over 25 years ago, he had to have his quince jelly. I could not find it in the supermarket and did not have a clue as to what a quince was. I found out that his father, Stanley Jorgensen, made quince jelly—of course, with the help of Edna Jorgensen. I decided I had better learn to make quince jelly or Bill would never be happy. We found a quince tree near the old cabin up at Dick and Ione's on Mines Road. Every year until we got our own tree established, we would make the trip to Dick and Ione's around September to pick quince for our year's supply of jelly. It was always great fun, and Ione always had something really good for lunch and wonderful people to visit with. Our method for cooking the quince in a slow cooker makes the job much easier, and Bill eats quince jelly on everything—even garlic bread.

CAROL JORGENSEN

5 pint canning jars, rings and lids

7 cups quince juice, from about
    10 large quinces
1 (1.75-ounce) package Sure-Jell
    light pectin
9 cups sugar

Scrub the quinces with a scrub brush. Cut them into small pieces (do not peel), and remove the seeds and cores. Place the chopped quince in a 4- or 5-quart slow cooker (they should fill it to the top). Cover the quinces with water, cover the pot, and cook on low for approximately 8 hours or until the fruit is dark pink. Drain the liquid from the fruit and set aside. Do not crush the fruit or use any of the pulp, which is all discarded now.

Prepare the jars and lids as described on page 67 so they will be ready when needed.

In a large pot, add 7 cups of quince juice and stir in the pectin. On high heat, bring the mixture to a full rolling boil, stirring constantly.

Add all of the sugar quickly to the juice mixture. Return to a full rolling boil and boil exactly 1 minute, stirring constantly. Remove the pot from the heat, skim off any foam, and immediately fill the jars with the liquid. Place the lids on tightly, place jars into a boiling water bath, and process for about 10 minutes. Remove, and allow to cool thoroughly.

After the jars have cooled, check the seals by pressing the middle of the lid with your finger. If the lid springs up when released, the lid is not sealed. Jars that have not sealed properly must be refrigerated and used within 3 weeks.

The Jorgensen family
Left to right: Lynn, Carol and
Bill, Carl, Edna, Shannon, and Cindy

Dressings,
Sauces, and
Marinades

Mona and Les Holm Sr.
The "Little House" at Fair View

Les Holm Sr.
as a toddler

American Art Studio. LIVERMORE, CAL.

Circle H ranchers
Les Holm Jr. and Les Holm Sr.

Tom Holm,
Les Jr.'s son and
Les Sr's grandson

Back: Frank Holm holding Gary
Holm, Les Holm Jr., Ben Benthien,
Lois Hansen Holm. Front: Patsy
Holm Neely, Bobby Holm, Ione Teeter
Holm, Tilli Holm Calhoun, Tom Holm,
Gladys Holm Benthien

Picnicking at Del Valle Creek
Annie Ibarolle, Les Holm Sr,
the Packard girl, Dick Holm,
Mona Detjens, Zoe Detjens, and
Bill Kaiser

Carl and Mabel Jorgensen, Stanley and
Phyllis Jorgensen, Art and Sophie Holm, Velma
and Verda Holm, Carl and Ida Holm, Dick
Holm, Billie Brown, Les Holm Sr. before
leaving for France to serve in World War I

Orange Salad Dressing

Makes about ¾ cup

My favorite salad to serve with this dressing is made with red and green curly lettuce, sliced green onions, mandarin orange slices, sliced mushrooms marinated in wine vinegar and lemon juice, and toasted sunflower seeds, almonds, or pecans.

PATSY HOLM NEELY

⅓ cup vegetable oil

3 tablespoons orange juice

3 tablespoons white wine vinegar

1 teaspoon Dijon style mustard

1 teaspoon seasoned salt

¼ teaspoon basil, crumbled

⅛ teaspoon pepper

Combine all the ingredients in a small bowl. Cover and refrigerate.

French Dressing

Makes about 1 cup

IONE TEETER HOLM

1 (8-ounce) can tomato sauce

⅔ cup oil

⅓ cup white wine vinegar

1 tablespoon minced onion

1 teaspoon salt

1 teaspoon Worcestershire sauce

½ teaspoon dry mustard

½ teaspoon paprika

1 clove garlic, minced

Combine all the ingredients in a container with a tight-fitting lid. Put on the lid and shake well. Store in the refrigerator.

Newlyweds Dick and Ione Holm in Santa Monica on their honeymoon, April 1926

Dick Holm, Bill Kilgo, Reba Kilgo, Kath Kilgo, Rich Holm

Green Goddess Dressing

Makes about 2 cups

REBA TEETER KILGO

A large handful of fresh parsley, finely chopped
1 green onion, including the green ends, finely chopped
4 to 5 young celery leaves, finely chopped
Pinch of fresh tarragon leaves, finely chopped
1 clove garlic, finely chopped
1½ cups mayonnaise
1 flat 2-ounce can anchovies, finely chopped with the oil
White vinegar, as needed

In a bowl, combine the parsley, onion, celery leaves, tarragon, and garlic. Add the mayonnaise and anchovies and mix well. Thin with vinegar until it reaches the desired consistency. Serve over romaine and chicory lettuce.

Roquefort Dressing

Makes 2 cups

This dressing is a tasty vinaigrette version, not the traditional creamy variety.

IONE TEETER HOLM

4 medium garlic cloves, minced
4 tablespoons olive oil
4 ounces Roquefort or other blue cheese
1 cup salad oil
½ cup cider vinegar
1 teaspoon salt
1 teaspoon paprika
½ teaspoon pepper

Combine all the ingredients in a container with a tight-fitting lid. Put on the lid and shake well. Store in the refrigerator.

Lou Gardella, Ione Holm, Edna Jorgensen, Dick Holm, Phyllis Fachner, Les Holm Sr. and Gladys Benthien

White Sauce (1888 Recipe)

Makes about 2½ cups

In the 1940s, we rode the school bus along Marina Avenue. As we neared South Livermore Avenue, we could see the colonial style house that my grandfather built for the Macleans. At the curve, the bus would stop to pick up Karl Wente. His mother had been my mother's home economics teacher at Livermore High School. Across the street lived Tressie Kirkman, my home economics teacher at Livermore High School. Both my mother and I learned to make this basic white sauce, which was a "must" for young women to know. The secret is straining to remove the lumps. You can add cream instead of milk, plus one beaten egg yolk—this is cream sauce.

MERILYN "TILLI" HOLM CALHOUN

¼ cup flour
¼ cup (½ stick) butter
Dash of grated nutmeg
Salt and pepper
2 cups milk

In a stew pan, combine the flour, butter, and nutmeg. Season with salt and pepper to taste. Mix well. Add the milk and stir constantly over the heat until the sauce thickens, about ten minutes. Strain through a medium mesh sieve.

Wente Road, Livermore

Original drawing of Wente Road, a portion of the Holm kids' school bus route, by Tilli Calhoun

Cranberry Sauce

Makes about 3 cups

IONE TEETER HOLM

4 cups fresh cranberries
1 cup water
1½ cups sugar

In a small pot over high heat, combine the cranberries and water and boil for 5 minutes. Push the mixture through a medium-mesh sieve over another pot to catch the liquid. Discard the skins. Add the sugar to the cranberry mash and boil for 5 more minutes. Pour the liquid into a decorative mold and chill overnight.

Christmas 1949
Sue Boies watches Ione
carve the turkey

Basic Vinaigrette

Makes 1 cup

1 teaspoon Dijon mustard
¼ cup red wine vinegar
¾ cup olive oil
1 clove garlic, peeled and
    finely chopped
Salt
Freshly ground black pepper
Sugar (optional)

In a small mixing bowl, whisk together the mustard and vinegar. Gradually whisk in the oil, then stir in the garlic, plus salt and pepper to taste. Taste for seasoning. If it is too oily, add more salt; if still too oily, add a pinch of sugar. For a thicker dressing, make it in a blender or food processor. It will keep in the refrigerator several weeks.

Granny had a drawer full of aprons, and she always wore one when she was cooking or working in the garden—a tradition lost by later generations.

Aprons

I don't think our kids know what an apron is. The principal use of Grandma's apron was to protect the dress underneath, but along with that…

It served as a potholder for removing hot pans from the oven.

It was wonderful for drying children's tears, and on occasion was even used for cleaning out dirty ears.

From the chicken coop, the apron was used for carrying eggs, fussy chicks, and sometimes half-hatched eggs to be finished in the warming oven.

When company came, those aprons were ideal hiding places for shy kids.

When the weather was cold, grandma wrapped it around her arms.

Those big old aprons wiped many a perspiring brow, bent over the hot wood stove.

Chips and kindling wood were brought into the kitchen in that apron.

From the garden, it carried all sorts of vegetables. After the peas had been shelled, it carried out the hulls.

In the fall, the apron was used to bring in apples that had fallen from the trees.

When unexpected company drove up the road, it was surprising how much furniture that old apron could dust in a matter of seconds.

When dinner was ready, Grandma walked out onto the porch, waved her apron, and the men knew it was time to come in from the fields to dinner.

It will be a long time before someone invents something that will replace that "old-time apron" that served so many purposes.

Life has changed – Grandma used to set her hot baked apple pies on the window sill to cool. Now, her granddaughters set theirs on the window sill to thaw.

—adapted from a poem by Tina Trivett

Venison Barbecue Sauce

Makes 1 gallon

The first hunter to kill a buck on the Circle H Ranch automatically knew that it had to be used for the annual deer barbecue. Sometimes it was the second buck, too—they did get smaller. No one particularly liked venison, so it was nice to know that the deer would be prepared using this sauce. This recipe was actually brother Jimmy's. After Jimmy died, Frank and others tried to make the barbecue sauce, but it was never as good as Jimmy's. In those days, exact measurements were never written down for recipes, and we relied solely on "taste testing." Usually, the venison was butchered into steaks and marinated overnight with this sauce. The weather for the barbecue was usually hot, so Frank's main job was to buy the beer, soda, and ice. An old cement double laundry tub located just outside the cabin was filled with ice. One side was used for the beer, one side for the soda. A coffee can was nailed to a nearby tree, and everyone was on the honor system to pay for drinks. At this point, everything was ready for the influx of family and friends who came for the big traditional Deer BBQ and a day of hashing over tales of old times and deer hunting. This was one of the biggest traditions of deer season in the Holm family. (Written by Joan Holm, Frank's wife)

FRANK HOLM

8 cups red wine
2 cups oil
2 (15-ounce) cans tomato sauce
Juice of 2 or 3 lemons
½ teaspoon pepper
½ teaspoon dry mustard
Cloves from 1 head of garlic, minced
½ onion, minced
1 tablespoon salt
1 shot glass (2 ounces) Worcestershire sauce
1 heaping teaspoon dried oregano
1 heaping teaspoon dried sweet basil

Frank Holm's sons, Gary and Dave

In a large nonreactive pot or bowl, combine all the ingredients, adding them in the order above. Let the mixture stand for 24 hours in the refrigerator. Add the venison pieces and marinate for 24 hours more, still in the refrigerator. Barbecue the meat outdoors—it's best at "the ranch." You can also use the marinade to baste the venison while it is cooking on the barbecue.

Granny's letter to Jimmy

Thursday, August 12, 1954
Corporal James G. Holm U.S. 56204606
10th Infantry Division
Fort Riley, Kansas

Dear Jimmy:

Well, the first blast of deer season is over and everyone is getting their second wind. The score to date—Blanche the first deer on the ranch; a forked horn weighing 90 lbs. at 7 a.m. They said they could hear her yelling all over the hills! She got it over at the corner of Section One. Lloyd Marsh, Jack Marino, Ed Ricketts, Tony, Hans Jensen (Carril's father), Roy Moore all got forked horns of various weights and Bill Marki (that friend of Tony's from South City) got two forks one right after the other, and Fred Shepherd's bro-in-law who is a cop in San Jose a 3-pointer and Tony a 3-pointer later in the day. He gave it to a young guy from Modesto who buys most of Dad's and Tony's calves—all these the first day on this side, and Don Hachman and Ed Spencer each got a forked horn over on the other side, and Charles Foxworthy, Clarence Groth, Tom Michell, and your good friend Cliff Jones all got fork horns on the other side. Richie had shooting 3 or 4 times, but the sight on Bro's gun is haywire so he left it down with Johnny George to be fixed.

Yesterday Dad, Gus Koopmann, Richie, Tony, Lloyd, and Joe Michell rode over almost to Tesla to move some cattle and then the rest, except Dad and Tony, who brought some cows and a steer on home, hunted up along Connolly's fence and around Mule Foot Rock. Richie got some shooting again but got his gun and the reins all tangled up and his foot caught in the stirrup and finally he just fell off Choppo. Then he had the gun up and aimed at a deer, pulled the trigger, and there was no shell in place. Slight case of buck fever probably complicated things, too. He sure was disgusted but is going back again with Lloyd tomorrow. Today, he, Dad, and Gus are putting some more 4-inch pipes in cement for posts around the corral. We just had lunch, they had their beauty naps and have gone to finish—I think they have 3 more holes to fill with rocks and cement. Dad was saying that if anyone ever wants to change the corral fences, they will sure cuss as those posts are in cement blocks about 30 inches deep by 24 inches square. Don't think the bulls can move the fences now. Blanche, Tony, and Lloyd went with Borges up to his ranch to hunt this a.m.

Bet Joe Michell is eating off the mantel today as they left here on horseback about 6:30 a.m. and didn't get back until 5 p.m., and he looked kind of tired but sure enjoyed his ride, and so did poor old Gus—he thanked Dad about ten times for taking him on such a nice ride.

Front to back: Jimmy, Tilli, and Frank Holm, Carl Stebbins, Bobby Holm, Leslie Holm, Louis Gardella, Jr.

Last nite Gus took Dad and I, Tony, Blanche, Sophie, Gladys, Ben, Mona and Les to Croce's near Lodi for dinner—a regular Italian dinner with a salad that you would have loved—about everything you can imagine in it. Sophie, Gus, and I had squab stuffed with wild rice and the rest had steak—I'm still full from it. Dad drove going over and I drove coming back—we got back up here about a quarter of twelve, and Tony and all had to get up about five I think—bet they are sleepy about now.

Guess Brother won't get any hunting after all, as in his last letter he said his replacement would probably come in by boat. He would come out on the same one. Joan says the trip is 18 days each way although that seems an awfully longtime. Anyway, he was very disgusted and still doesn't know where he will be stationed.

Dad and I had to go down Tuesday and cut up those lambs and put them in the freezer and then went down to take Joan's birthday presents to her—I got some stockings for you and Richie to give her so don't be surprised if you get a note thanking you for them. You should have seen Gary—he was just one big grin surrounded by chocolate cake which he had been eating. He is starting to talk like everything—said "vacuum cleaner" and then showed me where it was and was saying "moon" and trying to show it to Dad in the middle of the afternoon. You can imagine Joan's state of mind over Frank's delay getting home, as she thought sure he would be home the first of Sept.

Junie Rasmussen was home last weekend and is going to be sent to Virginia to quarter-master school, he thinks. Pretty good, huh? Guess Arry was his usual "happy self" over at the camp, as Richie said they didn't get to sleep until 3:30 Sat. a.m. and were up at 5.

Patsy started to work for Dr. Fraser yesterday as office nurse and was pretty scared about it. She was nervous anyway as some man backed out from the curb Monday and hit the fender of Hank's car. Did at least $50 damage. She and Hank killed a rattlesnake when they went down Sunday nite—only three rattles but they were real proud of themselves. Kay Stone had a baby boy either Sat. or Sun. Weighed almost eight pounds.

Glad you finally got some cool weather. It was quite cool and foggy here this a.m.—we've had breakfast in the kitchen the last three mornings but last weekend was pretty warm.

Blanche is going to bar-b-cue her deer this Sunday, so there will be a mob here. Hope the weather is nice for it.

Wayne didn't get a deer but his father got two nice ones. He and Sis are coming up here next week as he still has a week's vacation and she is thru with her job this Friday. She was sure surprised at the shower last Friday that Shirley gave—I sure did some fancy lying.

Love from all,

Mom

Ken's Turkey Marinade
Makes 1 gallon

I use this marinade when I cook turkey "my own special way."

KEN CALHOUN

1 tablespoon finely chopped fresh sage
Cloves from 1 large head garlic, peeled and finely chopped
1 bunch fresh parsley, finely chopped
½ cup salt
2 tablespoons pepper
1 gallon white wine
Juice from 3 lemons
1 cup olive oil

In a large bowl, combine the sage, garlic, parsley, salt, and pepper. Mix in the wine and lemon juice, then whisk in the oil.

Ken's Special Way *An extra refrigerator makes this easier. The turkey soaks in the great flavors as it marinates. I use a sixteen-pound turkey or smaller. A bigger bird is ok, but cooking times will be different. Depending on weight and heat, figure about twenty minutes per pound. Please don't overcook the bird—use a thermometer to be safe. If you use a gas grill, a three-burner grill with the middle burner turned off is great. Cook at 325°F to 350°F.*

Put a large plastic bag inside a tall plastic bucket or container. Pour the marinade into the bag. Place the turkey in the bag, pull up the sides, and tie the top, trying to submerge as much of the bird as possible. Refrigerate for 2 to 3 days, turning once a day. When ready to cook, prepare an indirect fire on a charcoal grill. Place the bird on the grill, cover, and cook for about 3 to 4 hours. There is no need to baste the turkey while cooking. Add more charcoal as needed (about 18 to 20 briquettes every hour) to maintain an even heat. The turkey is done when your thermometer reaches 165°F.

Meat and Game Marinade
Makes about 1¼ cups

When we were growing up, we used to have meat marinated in this recipe, especially when Dad would go deer hunting. It was so good with fresh venison, but you can also marinate a whole flank steak or tri-tip and then barbecue it. Dad would cut the meat into two-inch cubes, coat it well with the marinade, and let it sit in the refrigerator for at least six hours. Overnight is best. When it is done, be sure to slice the meat on the diagonal. Besides grilling, try dredging cubes of marinated meat in flour and frying them in oil, turning once, until done.

BECKY CALHOUN FOSTER

¾ cup salad oil
2 tablespoons red wine vinegar
¼ cup soy sauce
½ teaspoon ground ginger
3 tablespoons honey
½ teaspoon garlic powder
3 cloves garlic, minced (optional)

In a nonreactive pot or bowl, whisk together the oil, vinegar, soy sauce, ginger, honey, garlic powder, and garlic.

Gladys Holm Stebbins Benthien

Soups, Salads, and Sandwiches

Ben Benthien, Gladys
Holm Benthien, and Carl
Stebbins

Carl Stebbins,
circa 1928

Frank Holm and Carl
Stebbins, ROTC

July '29

Neil and Carl Stebbins

Carl Stebbins in his Coast
Guard uniform in front of the
Benthien house on the Holm
family's Fair View farm

Iris Murray Stebbins and
daughter Carla at the
Benthien house

Carla Stebbins Canter,
Jon Stebbins, and
Tina Stebbins Barbera

Country Pea Soup

Serves 6

This is one of my favorite winter soups. The original recipe came from Gloria Taylor at Retzlaff Estate Winery in Livermore. I beg, borrow, and steal leftover ham bones to make this if I don't have any of my own. I've also used frozen ham bones and even bacon. The recipe can be doubled easily, too. This soup can also be made in a slow cooker, cooking it all day. I use frozen meat when I use this method.

NANCY CALHOUN MUELLER

1 pound dried green split peas

6 to 7 cups water

¼ cup Chardonnay (optional)

1 leftover ham bone or ½ pound bacon

3 cloves garlic, finely minced

1 onion, coarsely chopped

3 to 4 potatoes, coarsely chopped

4 to 5 carrots, peeled and coarsely
     chopped

Handful fresh parsley, finely chopped

Pinch of cayenne pepper

1 bay leaf

2 whole cloves

Salt and freshly ground black pepper

Rinse the split peas in a strainer. In a large soup pot over high heat, combine the peas, water, and Chardonnay and bring to a boil. Add the ham bone, garlic, onion, potatoes, carrots, parsley, cayenne, bay leaf, and cloves. Season to taste with salt and pepper. Reduce the heat to medium-low and simmer, covered, for 1½ to 2 hours. Stir occasionally.

Remove the pot from the heat. Discard the bay leaf. Remove the ham bone and shred the meat from the bone, discarding any excess fat. Return the meat to the soup. Taste, correct the seasonings, and serve.

*Bob Taylor, Jennifer Marx,
Susie Calhoun, Gloria Taylor*

Bob and Gloria Taylor opened Retzlaff Estate Winery in the early 1980s. Bob and Gloria had invited family and friends to come help harvest the grapes. Susie Calhoun and her father, Wayne, helped out at one of the harvests and "recovered" at the party that followed. After a day of rounding up grapes, everyone enjoyed a barbecue and some wine, much like at the cattle roundups. The main differences were that we drank wine instead of whiskey—and there were no mountain oysters.

The Livermore Rodeo Kids Parade
Mona Holm, Bobby Holm, Carl
Stebbins, Jimmy Holm in wagon,
and Frank Holm behind wagon,
circa 1936

The annual rodeo parade was an
anticipated event for the Holm
family. The Circle H Ranch Riders
would saddle up early in the morning,
trailer the horses to town, ride in the
parade, and return via hoof to the
ranch. In Holm tradition, Ione was
in the kitchen preparing her special
shrimp, ham, and egg sandwiches.
The sandwiches, along with her iced
tea, were devoured by the family
during the lunch gathering at
the Calhouns' house after the
parade and before the rodeo.

Gazpacho

Serves 8

We served this soup icy cold at the rodeo parade picnic.

SMALL CAPS *Patsy Holm Neely*

4 cups tomato juice
2 beef bouillon cubes
2 tomatoes, peeled, seeded, and diced
½ cup peeled, seeded, and diced cucumber
½ cup seeded, diced green bell pepper
½ cup diced green onions
2 cloves garlic, minced
1 stalk celery, finely diced
¼ cup wine vinegar or freshly squeezed lime juice
2 tablespoons salad oil
1 teaspoon Worcestershire sauce
6 drops Tabasco sauce
Salt and pepper

The Holm kids: Leslie Jr., Bobby,
Frank, Carl Stebbins, Shirley
Miller, Tilli, Richie, and Jimmy

In a soup pot, bring the tomato juice to a boil. Add the bouillon cubes and stir until dissolved. Remove the pot from the heat and cool. Add the tomatoes, cucumber, bell pepper, green onions, garlic, celery, vinegar, oil, Worcestershire sauce and Tabasco sauce to the cooled broth. Season with salt and pepper to taste. Refrigerate until cold. Serve in chilled bowls.

Back seat: Merril Groth,
Frank Holm, and Don Baxter
Front seat: Neil Rasmussen,
Russ Rasmussen, and Don Cole

Circle H Ranch Riders
Merry Calhoun, Dave
Holm, Wendy Neely, and
Chad South, 1970

Kenny's Chinese Chicken Salad

Serves 4

KENNY CALHOUN

Dressing

¼ cup vegetable oil

4 tablespoons Japanese rice vinegar

4 tablespoons sugar

1 tablespoon salt

¼ teaspoon pepper

Salad

4 chicken breasts, cooked and shredded

1 large head iceberg lettuce, cut into thin strips

3 green onions, sliced

1 package Top Ramen Noodles, broken into small pieces **or**

⅓ package wonton skins, fried until crisp, and broken into small pieces

½ teaspoon sesame seeds, toasted

2 to 3 tablespoons slivered almonds, toasted

To make the dressing, whisk together the oil, vinegar, sugar, salt, and pepper. In a large salad bowl, mix together the chicken, lettuce, and green onions and toss with the dressing. When you are ready to serve, sprinkle the noodle pieces, sesame seeds, and almonds on top. Gently toss. (If you add these ingredients before you are ready to serve the salad, they will get soggy.)

Springtime at the Circle H Ranch
Lisa and Kenny Calhoun, 2007

Tahoe Clam Chowder

A fellow YACC (Young Adult Conservation Corp) member gave me this recipe while Bob and I were living in South Lake Tahoe, still newlyweds, and desperately in need of some recipes. We were living with our friend Patty Shirley, and after just three months of marriage, I had served some frightening meals.

NANCY CALHOUN MUELLER

Nancy Mueller and
Patty Shirley, 1982

   6 slices bacon, cut into ½-inch pieces
   2 carrots, coarsely chopped
   2 stalks celery, chopped
   1 yellow onion, chopped
   1 clove garlic, minced
   1½ pounds (about 4 or 5) potatoes, peeled and cut into ½-inch cubes
   2 (8-ounce) bottles clam juice
   8 (6.5-ounce) cans chopped clams
3 cups milk
½ teaspoon Tabasco sauce
¾ teaspoon fresh thyme leaves
1 bay leaf
Salt and pepper

Fry the bacon in the bottom of a 5-quart soup pot over medium heat. Leave about 2 table-spoons of the drippings in the pot. Add the carrots, celery, onion, and garlic and cook until lightly browned. Add the potatoes and clam juice. Bring to a boil, reduce the heat to low, and simmer until the potatoes are tender, about 15 minutes. Stir in the clams and their liquid, the milk, Tabasco, thyme, and bay leaf. Season with salt and pepper to taste. Heat until steaming and serve.

Cream of Pumpkin Soup

Serves 4

This soup is always a hit.

VICKIE REGNOLDS WARDEN

2 tablespoons butter
¼ cup finely chopped onion
1 teaspoon curry powder
1 tablespoon flour
1 (28-ounce) can chicken broth
1½ cups pumpkin purée
1 teaspoon brown sugar
⅛ teaspoon grated nutmeg
¼ teaspoon salt
⅛ teaspoon pepper
8 ounces cream cheese

Garnishes
Minced chives
Parsley
Sour cream

Melt the butter in the bottom of a 5-quart soup pot. Add the onion and sauté until soft. Stir in the curry powder and flour and cook until bubbling. Stir constantly to keep from burning, and whisk in the chicken broth. Stir in the pumpkin, sugar, nutmeg, salt, and pepper and bring the mixture to a simmer. Add the cream cheese. Carefully transfer the soup to a blender and purée. You may have to do this in batches. Return the soup to the pot and gently reheat. Serve, garnishing with minced chives, parsley, or sour cream.

Standing: Phyllis Fachner, Verda George, Mabel Rees, Tilli Holm, Bobby Holm, Otto Fachner, Gladys Benthien, Dick Holm, Ione Holm, Grandma Silver, Annie Holm, Walter Holm, Elvira Orloff, Betty Ann Orloff
Sitting: Dodo Cowell with Sandy and Sharon George, Patsy Holm, Richie Holm, Jim Holm

Carrot Soup

VICKIE REGNOLDS WARDEN

1 tablespoon butter plus 1½ tablespoons, melted
1 onion, chopped
1 small clove garlic, minced
2 carrots, finely sliced (about 1 cup)
4 cups chicken stock
Pinch of sugar
Salt and pepper
1 tablespoon cooked rice
1 tablespoon fresh mint, chopped
5 ounces milk

In the bottom of a pot over medium heat, melt 1 tablespoon butter. Add the onion, garlic, and carrots, and sauté until soft. Add the chicken stock and bring to a boil. Decrease the heat and simmer for 30 to 40 minutes. Refrigerate until cool.

Transfer the soup to a food processor, add the sugar, salt and pepper to taste. Add the melted butter, rice, and mint. Process until smooth. Return the soup to the pot and whisk in the milk. Stir constantly over medium heat until the soup is heated through.

Remembering Ione

The kitchen table has always been a place to share not only food but stories. On a daily basis, we would usually talk about the weather, the cattle, or the deer that were always eating the roses. After Papa died, it would be only Granny and I enjoying our breakfast. We would sit at the table, gazing at Cedar Mountain, sipping our coffee. This story is one that Granny shared with me about her mother, Hattie Puntney Teeter.

When Granny was a young girl, her father moved the family back to Arkansas to be close to Hattie's family. Hattie had been taken over by depression, and the hope was that she would improve being around her family. Things did not improve, and her father moved the four children back to Livermore. Hattie was eventually hospitalized and died in Arkansas. Granny never saw her again. She said this saddened her all her life, although she never let on.

I believe this experience is what gave her the strength to endure many more losses and hardships throughout her life. It also gave her the wisdom, as our matriarch, to let us know that we were each loved, and to value our family. She was accepting of all, and she had the integrity to always do what was right.

— Susie Calhoun

and Ione Holm to the World's Fair—her husband, Otto, had to work and missed the fun. Nearly seventy years later, Phyllis recalls the fair as being crowded, the exhibits very impressive, and the grounds beautiful. Dick, as usual, picked up the tab for lunch that day, and he mentioned he was afraid the cash register at the cafeteria would catch fire while the high-priced fair food was rung up. Unlike the comfortable and casual wear you would see at a similar event today, Phyllis and Ione wore dresses and heels to the World's Fair, and Dick wore a suit, hat, and tie.

Tilli Holm had the opportunity to go twice—once with the Maitland Henry family and again with her third-grade class, via a school bus. Her future husband, Wayne Calhoun, went five times. One was with the Alameda County Traffic Patrol, along with thousands of children from throughout Alameda County.

Continental Cauliflower Salad

Serves 8

This recipe is perfect for family picnics, and other gatherings.

GAYLE FACHNER DILTZ

4 cups thinly sliced cauliflower
½ to ¾ cup pitted black olives, sliced
½ green bell pepper, seeded and chopped
½ red bell pepper, seeded and chopped, or 1 (3.25-ounce) can chopped pimentos
½ cup chopped green onion
½ cup olive oil
3 tablespoons lemon juice
3 tablespoons red wine vinegar
1 teaspoon salt
½ teaspoon sugar
¼ teaspoon pepper
1 or 2 cloves garlic, minced (optional)

In a large salad bowl, combine the cauliflower, olives, peppers, and green onion. In a small bowl, combine the oil, lemon juice, vinegar, salt, sugar, and pepper; add garlic to taste and mix well. Pour the dressing over the vegetables and toss to combine. Cover and refrigerate for 4 hours or overnight. Overnight is best!

Granny and Papa's Summer Harvest Salad

We would have incredible lunches and dinners every weekend and many a week night at Granny and Papa's house. I especially enjoyed them in the summer when we would eat the fresh vegetables from their garden. I think my corn-on-the-cob eating record was five ears, and the string beans with red onion and bacon were to die for. We never realized how hard Papa worked and what a green thumb he had until he was gone. One of the simple and delicious salads Granny would always serve from Papa's garden was a cucumber, tomato, and red onion salad. I serve it all the time, and everyone loves it. To add a fresh zing, I add thinly sliced fresh basil.

NANCY CALHOUN MUELLER

Cucumbers, peeled and sliced
Tomatoes, sliced
Red onions, sliced
White vinegar
Salt and pepper

Mix the vegetables together with a few tablespoons of vinegar. Season with salt and pepper to taste, and, voila—there you have it!

Agurkesalat (Danish Sliced Cucumbers in Vinegar)   *Serves 12*

Slender, solid cucumbers with the fewest seeds are best for this salad.

MERILYN "TILLI" HOLM CALHOUN

4 cucumbers
1 tablespoon salt
¾ cup vinegar
2 tablespoons sugar
⅛ teaspoon pepper
1 tablespoon chopped fresh parsley,
   optional

Peel the cucumbers (this is optional) and slice them into ⅛-inch rounds into a bowl; sprinkle with salt. Place a weight on top of them for 1 to 2 hours, pressing out the juice and removing the bitter taste. In a small bowl or jar, combine the vinegar, sugar, and pepper. Drain the cucumbers and dress them with the vinegar mixture. Chopped parsley may be added, if desired.

To save time, try this shortcut: Put the sliced cucumbers into a jar with salt. Shake well, drain off the liquid, and season the cucumbers with the vinegar mixture. However, the first method is preferable.

Broccoli Salad

MERRY "LAMBIE" CALHOUN CARTER

Serves 4 to 6

Dressing

⅔ cup mayonnaise

⅔ cup sugar, or less

2 tablespoons red wine vinegar

Salad

4 cups uncooked chopped broccoli

1 cup raisins

1 small onion, chopped

8 slices bacon, cooked and crumbled

1 cup sunflower seeds, pine nuts,
    cashews, or slivered almonds

Prepare the dressing by combining the mayonnaise, sugar to taste, and vinegar in a small bowl or jar.

In a bowl, combine the broccoli, raisins, and onion. Add the dressing and toss. Just before serving, add the bacon and nuts and toss again.

*Merry Carter with daughters
Whitney and Laina*

Granny's Tomato Aspic

IONE TEETER HOLM

Serves 12

5½ cups tomato juice

3 (3-ounce) packages lemon Jell-o

2½ tablespoons vinegar

1 teaspoon Worcestershire sauce

Salt and pepper

1 cup diced celery

1 avocado, peeled, seeded, and diced

2 green onions, diced

½ pound shrimp

In a saucepan over medium heat, combine the tomato juice, Jell-o, vinegar, and Worcestershire sauce. Season with salt and pepper to taste. Stir until the Jell-o dissolves and the mixture comes to a boil. Remove from the heat and let it cool. Add the celery, avocado, green onions, and shrimp. Pour into an 8-cup mold. Refrigerate until set, then unmold and serve.

Taco Salad à la Polly

Serves 8 to 10

This salad has become my ticket in the door to "Easter in the Hills." The dressing recipe came from a friend, and the dressing is what gives the salad its tangy flavor.

POLLY SVEEN GALLAGHER

Salad
1 pound ground beef
1 (1.25-ounce) package taco seasoning
1 head iceberg lettuce, chopped
¾ pound Cheddar cheese, shredded
3 tomatoes, chopped

Dressing
1 (10.75-ounce) can tomato soup
¾ cup salad oil
½ cup apple cider vinegar
1 teaspoon dry mustard
1 teaspoon Worcestershire sauce
¼ teaspoon salt
1 cup sugar

½ (11-ounce) package tortilla chips, crumbled

In a frying pan over medium heat, brown the ground beef. Drain the grease if necessary. Mix in the taco seasoning.

In a large bowl, toss together the lettuce, cheese, and tomatoes. Add the ground beef and toss again.

Using a blender or food processor, blend together the soup, oil, vinegar, mustard, Worcestershire sauce, salt, and sugar.

Just before serving, add the tortilla chips to the salad mixture. Pour approximately half the dressing over the salad, toss, and serve.

Brett Holm's graduation from the Firefighters Academy on Oahu: Polly and Vince Gallagher, Teri, Brett, and Gary Holm

Korinne's Taco Salad

Serves 8 to 10

KORINNE DILTZ

1 pound lean ground beef
1 (1.25-ounce) package taco seasoning
1 head iceberg lettuce, chopped
2 cups Cheddar cheese, shredded
1 (14-ounce) can kidney beans, drained
1 red onion, chopped
1 (2.25-ounce) can sliced black olives
1 avocado, peeled, seeded and diced
2 medium tomatoes, chopped
½ (11-ounce) package tortilla chips, crumbled
1 (8-ounce) bottle Kraft Catalina dressing

In a frying pan over medium heat, brown the ground beef. Drain the grease if necessary. Mix in the taco seasoning. Let cool.

In a large bowl, combine the lettuce, cheese, beans, onion, olives, avocado, and tomato. Toss to combine.

Just before serving, add the meat and chips to the salad mixture, then pour the dressing over the top and toss. Serve immediately.

Tortellini Spinach Salad

Serves 4

JANET FACHNER VON TOUSSAINT

1 (6-ounce) bag ready-to-serve spinach
1 (9-ounce) package cheese, garlic or herb tortellini (from the refrigerator case), cooked, drained, and cooled
2 to 3 chopped green onions
6 to 8 slices bacon, crisp-fried, drained, and crumbled (use more or less to your liking)
½ small basket cherry tomatoes, halved
Reduced-fat ranch dressing

In a salad bowl, combine the spinach, tortellini, green onions, and bacon. Just before serving, add the tomatoes and toss with enough dressing just to coat.

*The Fachners
Back: Danny Fachner
Front: Janet Von Toussaint, Phyllis Fachner, Gayle Diltz*

Granny's Potato Salad

An excerpt from Granny's diary:

"July 4, 1971. Nice day. Up at 6 to make 14 lbs. salad. Dick over to lay fire sprinkler, etc. Rich took me over to put oilcloth on tables, etc. G & Ben not here. 96 of us, very good day, home about 9."

Lori Neely South would help Granny make her large batches of potato salad. This recipe was never written down; therefore the amounts are estimates. This recipe calls for five pounds of potatoes and serves a crowd of about twenty. For Easter and the Fourth of July, Granny always used twelve to fifteen pounds of potatoes.

IONE TEETER HOLM

French dressing
1 cup salad oil

4 tablespoons red wine vinegar

4 tablespoons lemon juice

4 teaspoons sugar

1 teaspoon salt

1 teaspoon Spice Islands paprika

1 teaspoon dry mustard

Salad
5 pounds red potatoes, cooked
    and peeled

Salt and pepper

5 stalks celery, finely chopped

1 red onion, finely chopped

Best Foods mayonnaise

Miracle Whip salad dressing

To make the dressing, combine the oil, vinegar, lemon juice, sugar, salt, paprika, and dry mustard in a jar with a tight-fitting lid. Cover and shake well.

Thinly slice about 3 potatoes and put them in a mixing bowl. Add a dash of salt and pepper, sprinkle with the dressing, and mix well. Add approximately a ¼ cup of the celery and ¼ of the red onion; mix again. Add approximately 3 heaping tablespoons of the mayonnaise and 2 heaping tablespoons of the Miracle Whip salad dressing; mix again. Transfer this batch to a large mixing bowl. Repeat this same process until all the potatoes are used, being sure to mix the batches together as they are added to the larger mixing bowl.

Chill for 1 to 2 hours before serving.

The Holm family and friends at the Livermore Rodeo Parade, 2007

Shrimp Macaroni Salad

Serves 4

This salad can be made the night before serving.

BONNIE HOWE

1 (16-ounce) package salad macaroni (large pasta shells), cooked and drained
½ cup Gerard's Italian salad dressing
1 pound large shrimp
1 cup diced green onion
½ teaspoon salt
½ teaspoon pepper
1 cup Best Foods mayonnaise
½ cup chili sauce

In a bowl, marinate the macaroni in the salad dressing for at least 1 hour; overnight is best. Add the shrimp, onion, salt, and pepper; toss to combine.

Combine the mayonnaise and chili sauce in a small bowl. When you are ready to eat, add it to the salad, toss well and serve.

Bonnie, Wendy, Warren, and Bob Howe
June 3, 1978

Remembering *Ma* (Ione)

As a kid we always ate well, but there were three dishes that stand out in my mind; Ma put her own signature on them. They were her spaghetti, her potato salad and her brownies. Maybe I preferred them because we grew up with them.

The spaghetti was made with a lot of sauce, a lot of ground beef, and garlic. I don't know what other ingredients she used, but they filled the house with a great aroma. It not only smelled good, it tasted great.

Her potato salad was my favorite. Most of the family doesn't like eggs, so there were none in her salad. She also used something in the dressing that turned it pink. The onion and garlic were finely minced. What else went in the dressing I don't know, but the salad seemed to improve with time. Because it took time to make, it was only made on special occasions. Maybe that's what made it especially good.*

Most brownies are cake-like. Ma's were more cookie-like. They were made for special occasions, too.

Ma was a good cook. These three favorites seemed to me to be one step above the rest.

— *Richard Holm*

Artichoke Rice Salad

Serves 6

This recipe was given to my mother by my cousin Joanie Nielsen. We have been serving it for years, and it is still a family favorite. You can add cooked shrimp to the salad to serve it as a main dish.

IRIS MURRAY STEBBINS

1 (6.9-ounce) package reduced-sodium chicken Rice-a-Roni

2 green onions, chopped

½ green bell pepper, chopped

2 (6.5-ounce) jars marinated artichoke hearts, drained and chopped

8 stuffed green olives, sliced

½ cup sliced celery

1 (4-ounce) can sliced button mushrooms

⅓ cup mayonnaise (do not use low-fat version)

½ teaspoon curry powder

Salt and pepper

Cook the Rice-a-Roni the day before and chill it overnight. The next day, add the onions, bell pepper, artichoke hearts, olives, celery, and mushrooms and mix well. Stir in the mayonnaise; season with curry powder and salt and pepper to taste. Chill thoroughly before serving.

Iris Stebbins, Don Ousley, Tina Barbera, Joelle Barbera Dills, Richard Dills, Carl Stebbins

Dinner Club in the Benthien–Stebbins cabin at Lake Almanor: the Stebbins, the Calhouns, the Devanys, the Keenes, and the Bittencourts

Summer Pasta Salad

This is a great summer salad, the fresh veggies are real tasty. I sometimes add mushrooms, zucchini, and fresh basil. You can use any fresh vegetables you like. It makes a lot and keeps well. And of course, it's easy!

BECKY CALHOUN FOSTER

1 pound spaghetti

1 cup Italian salad dressing with herbs

1 bell pepper (red, green, or yellow), cut into ½-inch dice

2 tomatoes, cut into ½-inch dice

1 cucumber, sliced

1 small red onion, cut into ½-inch dice

2 tablespoons grated Parmesan cheese

4 tablespoons McCormick Salad Supreme seasoning

Cook the spaghetti according to the package instructions; drain. Transfer to a bowl and add the salad dressing. Toss well to coat. When the spaghetti has cooled, add the bell pepper, tomatoes, cucumber, onion, and cheese. Last, add the salad seasoning. Marinate at least several hours or overnight before serving.

Warm Spinach and Basil Salad

Serves 6

I made this for an Italian-themed gourmet dinner. It is so good! Honestly, it's one of the best salads I've ever had.

BECKY CALHOUN FOSTER

6 cups fresh spinach leaves

2 cups fresh basil leaves (1 large bunch)

½ cup best-quality olive oil

3 cloves garlic, finely chopped

½ cup pine nuts

4 ounces prosciutto, diced

Salt and freshly ground black pepper

¾ cup freshly grated Parmesan cheese

Toss the spinach and basil together in large salad bowl. Heat the oil in a medium-sized skillet over medium heat. Add the garlic and pine nuts and sauté until the nuts begin to brown slightly. Stir in the prosciutto and cook 1 more minute. Season to taste with salt and pepper. Pour the warm oil-prosciutto mixture over the spinach and basil, and toss. Sprinkle the salad with the Parmesan. Serve immediately and pass the pepper mill.

Savory Ham Sandwiches

Makes 16 sandwiches

MERILYN "TILLI" HOLM CALHOUN

¼ cup (½ stick) softened butter or margarine
2 tablespoons yellow mustard, plus more for garnish
16 thin slices pumpernickel bread (about 3 inches square)
1 pound sliced ham
2 to 3 hard-cooked eggs, sliced
4 to 6 radishes, sliced
Chopped fresh parsley, for garnish

Combine the butter and mustard in a small bowl. Spread each slice of bread with the mixture; place 1 or 2 pieces of ham on top of each slice, dividing the ham evenly. Top with the egg and radish slices. Garnish with chopped parsley or a piping of yellow mustard.

Cheese and Ham Sandwiches

Makes 16 sandwiches

MERILYN "TILLI" HOLM CALHOUN

16 thin slices pumpernickel bread (about 3 inches square)
¼ cup (½ stick) softened butter or margarine
1 pound sliced Havarti cheese
½ pound sliced ham
Radish slices, for garnish

Lightly spread the bread slices with butter. Divide the cheese and ham slices among the bread. Garnish with radish slices.

DANSK SMØRREBRØD
(Danish open-faced sandwiches)

Open-faced sandwiches are well-known Danish fare and are perfect for entertaining as they can be made ahead of time and refrigerated. In Denmark, the sandwiches are usually made on thin slices of buttered black bread, but we generally make them on rye, pumpernickel, white, sourdough, and wheat bread. The sandwiches are arranged and served on platters garnished with parsley, radishes, and dill. Plan on a minimum of three sandwiches for each guest.

Livermore Dania Hall dedication (Carl Holm with white beard, middle of the front row) 1911

FORSLAG TIL DANSK SMØRREBRØD (Suggestions for Danish open-faced sandwiches)

You can create your own recipes with the ingredients listed below. Make the sandwiches on thinly sliced and halved buttered bread. Meats and vegetables should be thinly sliced, also.

Fish and shellfish – shrimp, smoked salmon, caviar, anchovies, herring

Meats – roasted beef, pork, or lamb; ham, smoked duck

Egg – hard-boiled, chopped or sliced; scrambled

Cheeses – Gorgonzola, blue cheese, grated Parmesan, Brie

Vegetables – beets, onions, spinach, mushrooms, cucumbers, asparagus, radishes, tomatoes

Condiments and garnishes – capers, chives, dill, fresh parsley, rémoulade, mayonnaise, mustard, creamed horseradish

Reter (Tiny Shrimp) Sandwiches

Makes 16 sandwiches

MERILYN "TILLI" HOLM CALHOUN

2 (1-pound) packages frozen, shelled, deveined shrimp, thawed
6 tablespoons mayonnaise or salad dressing
2 tablespoons lemon juice plus more for drizzling
1 teaspoon fresh dillweed
16 slices of pumpernickel bread (about 3 inches square)
Lemon peel twists, for garnish

Cook and drain the shrimp. If they are large, chop them into bite-sized pieces. Chill thoroughly before proceeding.

In a small bowl, combine the mayonnaise, lemon juice, and dillweed. Spread evenly on the slices of bread. Top with the shrimp, dividing it evenly among the slices. Drizzle with lemon juice and garnish with the lemon twists.

Tilli's Shrimp Salad Spread

Makes about ¾ cup

I find it helps to freeze the bread, then lightly butter it to prevent soggy sandwiches. You can also use fresh shrimp instead of canned.

MERILYN "TILLI" HOLM CALHOUN

1 (4.5-ounce) can shrimp, drained, patted dry, and chopped
Fresh squeezed lemon juice
1 small green onion, green and white parts, finely chopped
1 celery stalk, finely chopped
Pepper
¼ cup mayonnaise, plus more if needed

Place the shrimp in a small bowl, sprinkle with lemon juice to taste, and toss. Gently mix in the onion and celery. Season with pepper to taste. Blend in the mayonnaise. If needed, add more mayonnaise to make the mixture spreadable.

Patsy's Curried Chicken Sandwich Spread

Makes 4 cups spread

PATSY HOLM NEELY

1 (3-pound) whole chicken, cut into pieces

1 bay leaf

1 onion, cut in half

⅓ cup Wish-bone light red wine vinegar
salad dressing, more if needed

1 to 2 stalks celery, very finely chopped

1 cup green onion, white and green parts,
finely sliced

1 teaspoon curry powder

½ cup currants

½ cup pecans or other nuts, toasted, finely
chopped

1 cup mayonnaise

½ cup Miracle Whip

1 (4-ounce) container alfalfa sprouts

Place the chicken in a large pot, cover with water, add the bay leaf and onion, and bring to a boil. Decrease the heat and simmer until tender, about 1 hour. (Cooking time will vary depending on the size and age of your chicken.) Drain and pat the chicken parts dry. Pull the meat from the bones and cut into bite-size pieces. Place the chicken in a shallow dish and toss with the red wine vinegar dressing. Cover and marinate overnight in the refrigerator.

The next day, combine the chicken with the celery, green onion, curry, currants, nuts, mayonnaise, and Miracle Whip. Serve on slices of dark rye and garnish with the sprouts.

Back: Mabel Holm Jorgensen Rees, Grace Gardella, Margaret Baxter, Mona Detjens Holm Front: Phyllis Jorgensen Fachner, Gladys Holm Benthien, Janet and Danny Fachner, Bobby Holm

Remembering Ida

I remember my grandmother, Ida Holm, as a very loving and charitable person. Her favorite pastime was preparing for a church benefit, rummage sale, or bazaar.

Grandma was chairman of "The Country Store" booth at the yearly church bazaar. Prepared food items were sold at this booth. A favorite food item was Grandma's homemade Danish pickles (see recipe on page 69).

"Snowballs" were a special treat she served on Christmas Eve. Grandma made a white cake from scratch, baked the batter in her aebleskiver pan, then turned them upside down and frosted them individually with a white almond frosting.

Such wonderful memories of a very special grandmother.

— Phyllis Fachner

108

Spam and Egg Sandwich Spread

Makes about 2 cups

PHYLLIS JORGENSEN FACHNER

1 (12-ounce) can Spam Lite, chopped

3 sweet pickles, chopped

2 or 3 hard-boiled eggs, chopped

⅓ cup chopped black olives

¼ cup mayonnaise, plus more as needed

In a bowl, combine the Spam, pickles, eggs, and olives. Stir in the mayonnaise. You may have to add a little more mayonnaise to make the mix spreadable.

Jake and Mabel Rees,
Otto and Phyllis Fachner

Egg Salad Sandwiches

Makes 12 sandwiches

Luncheon or tea sandwiches have always been a tradition at Holm Christmas Eve open house. This recipe was one of Granny's staples. A bit of mustard adds zip.

IONE TEETER HOLM

1 dozen hard-boiled eggs, chopped

1 (2.25-ounce) can chopped olives

1 (4-ounce) can pimento, drained and chopped

3 or 4 small sweet pickles, finely chopped

1 stalk celery, finely chopped (optional)

2 tablespoons minced red onion (optional)

1 cup mayonnaise plus more as needed

Salt and pepper

2 tablespoons prepared mustard

24 slices white sandwich bread, crusts removed (12 slices if you prefer open-faced sandwiches)

In a bowl, combine the eggs, olives, pimento, pickles, celery, and onion. You can add more celery and onion to taste. Stir in the mayonnaise. You may need more to hold the mixture together when spread. Season with salt, pepper, and mustard to taste. Spread on 12 of the bread slices, top with the remaining slices of bread, and serve.

Easy Stuffed Rolls

Makes 24 rolls

PHYLLIS JORGENSEN FACHNER *originally from the kitchen of Hannah Faure*

1 (12-ounce) can Spam, chopped

¾ pounds sharp American cheese, shredded

1 (4-ounce) can Ortega peppers, chopped

1 (8-ounce) can tomato sauce

1 (2.25-ounce) can chopped black olives

24 hot dog buns

Preheat the oven to 350°F.

Mix together the Spam, cheese, and peppers. Transfer to a bowl and blend in the tomato sauce and olives. Scoop out the centers of the tops and bottoms of 24 hot dog buns and fill each side with a couple tablespoon of the mixture. Close together the top and bottom of each roll, wrap in foil, and place in a roasting pan with a cover. Cover and heat in the oven for 40 minutes or until the rolls are warmed through. Check occasionally to make sure they do not burn.

French Dip Sandwiches

Papa always enjoyed a good French dip sandwich; we would order them at Livermore Joe's on our Friday Holm family lunch excursions. I tasted this recipe at the home of my cousins, Jeff and Vicki Calhoun when we spent a weekend there. They are so easy, and so good—as good as Livermore Joe's if you ask me. I don't cook roast beef very well, so the only leftover beef we usually have is barbecued tri-tip, and it works great. Columbo Sour Sandwich Rolls are my favorite to use in this recipe.

NANCY CALHOUN MUELLER

Leftover roast beef

Sourdough rolls, sliced in half

Beef bouillon cubes

Butter

Thinly slice your leftover roast beef. Place it in a pan and cover with water. Add 1 bouillon cube per cup of water. Bring to a boil, and simmer on low for about 20 minutes.

Butter the rolls and brown them in a frying pan.

To serve, place a roll on each plate and layer the beef on top of the rolls. Pour the juice into individual serving bowls. Dip in and enjoy!

Leslie Calhoun, Nancy and Bob Mueller, and John Calhoun

Phyllis Jorgensen Fachner remembers

Ione was the most wonderful person. She was like a sister to me, and she was a fabulous cook. I remember Ione preparing hot lunches and taking them at noon to the men working farm equipment all over the countryside.

Ione was very family oriented. She was always fixing someone's hair. She would style the hair of her sisters-in-law Gladys, Mabel, and Mona. Ione made me feel so special when it was my turn.

I remember being at Fair View when there was a fire down the road at the old Inman Farm. When the fire jumped the tracks, Uncle Dick ran and got the harvester crew to help fight the fire. Meantime, Mona drove the car to pick up Dad and the men working on the harvest. Aunt Gladys was hanging from the running boards of the car. Ione and Grandma Ida were so worried. They went upstairs and changed into black dresses. Then they went outside, sat on the bench around the tree, and stayed there, frightened, holding hands, waiting to evacuate.

I was Ione's babysitter after high school. I tended to the children, and, for the men, baked Uncles' Special Cake. (See page 193.)

After I grew up and raised my own family, my husband, Otto, and I spent many memorable times with Ione and Dick. We took short trips, took turns hosting the bridge club with the family, and spent relaxing times just visiting. I remember Ione and Dick's kindness when Otto died in 1976. They checked in on me regularly, visited frequently, and spent time reminiscing.

The Holm family visits with Bob Holm, on leave from the Marines, at the "Little House" on the Fair View farm.
Back: Grampa Silver, Bob Holm (killed on Okinawa, May 1945), Sophia Holm, Otto Fachner, Phyllis Fachner, Annie Holm, Gladys Benthien, Mabel Rees, Les Holm Sr., Grandma Silver
Kneeling: Elvira Orloff, Ione Holm, Betty Ann Orloff
Front: Rich Holm, Shorty the dog, Patsy Holm

Ione Holm dressed to go riding

Not-So-Easy Stuffed Rolls

Makes 18 rolls

Here's another from Phyllis. She says it's good too, but a little more work than the Easy Stuffed Rolls on page 110.

PHYLLIS JORGENSEN FACHNER *originally from the kitchen of Leota O'Neil*

1 small onion

1 clove garlic

1 (4-ounce) can Ortega diced green chilies

8 hard-boiled eggs

3 sweet pickles

1 large slice cooked ham

½ cup black olives

¾ pounds sharp Cheddar cheese, finely grated

2 tablespoons vinegar

1 teaspoon Worcestershire sauce

1 teaspoon prepared mustard

2 tablespoons mayonnaise, or enough to hold mix together

Dash of cayenne red pepper

Salt and pepper

18 French rolls, with the centers scooped out (hot dog buns can also be used)

Preheat the oven to 300°F.

Grind or chop together the onion, garlic, chilies, eggs, pickles, ham, and olives. Place in a bowl and combine with the cheese. Add the vinegar, Worcestershire sauce, mustard, mayonnaise, and cayenne. Season with salt and pepper to taste. Mix thoroughly. Scoop a couple of tablespoons into the bottom of each roll. Top with the other half of the roll, wrap individually in foil, and pack into a covered roasting pan. Heat in the oven for 45 minutes. If the rolls were frozen when filling, heat at 350°F for 1 hour.

Annual Fachner family vacation at Monte Bella Court in Santa Cruz, 1958 Phyllis, Otto, Gayle, Danny, and Janet

At the beach in Santa Cruz Edna and Stanley Jorgensen, Coco Jorgensen Reynolds, and Phyllis Jorgensen Fachner

Chicken Roll-Ups

Serves 8

These are tasty for lunch or dinner. I have also made them smaller to use as appetizers. Depending on how much of the chicken mixture you use in each roll, you may need more croissants. The mixture does go a long way, and the assembled croissants freeze very well.

BECKY CALHOUN FOSTER

½ cup finely chopped walnuts

½ cup dried seasoned bread crumbs

½ cup margarine (¼ cup softened, ¼ cup melted), plus more as needed

1 (8-ounce) tub cream cheese with chives, at room temperature

3 cooked chicken breasts, cubed

¼ pound mushrooms, sliced and sautéed

6 green onions (including tops), chopped and sautéed

2 packages croissant rolls (8 per package)

Preheat the oven to 350°F.

Combine the nuts and the bread crumbs in a shallow dish and set aside. Blend the soft margarine with the cream cheese in a large bowl. Fold in the chicken, mushrooms, and onions. Carefully unroll each croissant roll so you have a flat, triangular piece of dough. Dip one side of the dough in the melted margarine, then the bread-nut mixture. Turn the dough over and place about ¼ cup of the chicken mixture in the center, then roll it up to form a cresent shape. Repeat with the remaining pieces of dough. Place the rolls on a cookie sheet and bake for 25 to 35 minutes, or until golden brown.

The Calhoun cousins, 1995
Becky Calhoun Foster, Nancy Calhoun Mueller, Cindy Calhoun Miller, Merry Calhoun Carter, Jeff, Susie, and Kenny Calhoun

Several members of the extended Holm family pursued nursing careers. Many of them attended Merritt Hospital's School of Nursing in Oakland.

Clockwise from upper left corner:
Mona Detjens, Millie Mohr, Gladys Holm Benthien
Coco Jorgensen Regnolds
Mona Detjens Holm – Gladys said the nurses called her "the Dresden doll"
Merritt Hospital in Oakland
Deanna Dickey Holm on left
Verda Holm George
Center: Nurse Ida Murray (Carl Stebbins' mother-in-law) holding newborn Susie Calhoun at St. Paul's Hospital in Livermore, 1954

Ione Teeter Holm and Dick Holm
Wedding Day, 1926

Baby Dick Holm

Grace and Lou Gardella
with Ione and Dick
Holm, 1975

Back: Tilli and Frank
Front: Patsy, Jimmy, and
Richie

The Cherubs with Granny and Papa
First Christmas in the new house on
Mines Road, 1966

Son Frank Holm toasts to
fifty years of wedded bliss
for Ione and Dick Holm

Papa and Susie Calhoun, 1956

Papa and Brett Holm

Santa Margarita Pasta

This is what we eat when it gets hot out here in the Santa Margarita hills. It looks a lot like Mines Road in Livermore where we lived for many years. This is a fast and easy recipe that can be served immediately or refrigerated for a picnic. Enjoy!

JON AND NADIA STEBBINS

4 tablespoons olive oil

2 sweet yellow Vidalia onions, cut into
    1-inch dice

2 skinless, boneless chicken breasts, cut
    into 1-inch dice

Salt and pepper

½ to ¾ teaspoon paprika

Pinch red pepper flakes

8 ounces penne pasta

6 cloves garlic

1 each red, green, and yellow bell peppers,
    seeded and cut into 1-inch dice

Parmesan cheese, grated, for garnish

The trick to this recipe is to have everything done cooking at the same time. In a pot over high heat, bring the pasta water to a boil. To cook the chicken and vegetables, I use 2 frying pans, adding 2 tablespoons of oil to each pan. Since the vegetables usually take a little longer, I start them first. Add the onion to one frying pan and cook until translucent, stirring frequently. While the onions are cooking, add the chicken to the second pan and sear on all sides before seasoning with salt, pepper, paprika, and red pepper. (Add more red pepper if you like.) Add the pasta to the boiling water when you start cooking the chicken. When the water returns to a boil, reduce the heat to a simmer and cook the pasta until al dente. While the pasta cooks, continue to sauté the chicken until it is no longer pink in the middle, about 10 minutes. Stir frequently.

When the onions are almost translucent, press the garlic through a garlic press into the onions. When the garlic just begins to brown, add the peppers and sauté until they have cooked but still have a little crunch to them; be careful not to overcook.

When the pasta is ready, drain it and turn it into a large bowl. Add the chicken and vegetables and toss thoroughly to coat the pasta with the sauces from both the chicken and the vegetables. Serve immediately, topped with grated Parmesan cheese.

The Stebbins family
Jon, Nadia, Shannon,
and Sophie

Country Vegetable Lasagna

Makes 6 servings

This is one of the best vegetarian lasagnas I've tasted.

SUSIE CALHOUN

2 tablespoons olive oil

½ pound mushrooms, sliced

2 large onions, finely chopped (about 2 cups)

3 cloves garlic, minced

6 large ripe tomatoes (about 2¼ pounds), peeled, and chopped or 3 (16-ounce) cans whole tomatoes, drained

½ cup Zinfandel

½ cup chopped fresh parsley

2 teaspoons salt

1 teaspoon dried basil, crumbled

½ teaspoon dried oregano, crumbled

¼ teaspoon grated nutmeg

¼ teaspoon dried thyme, crumbled

4 medium-size zucchini (about 1¼ pounds), sliced about ¼-inch thick

8 ounces lasagna noodles

Boiling salted water (with a few drops vegetable oil added)

1 pint ricotta cheese (about 1 pound)

¾ pound Monterey Jack cheese, shredded (about 3 cups)

½ cup grated Parmesan cheese

⅓ cup slivered almonds

Sliced black olives, for garnish

In a Dutch oven or large saucepan over medium heat, heat the oil and brown the mushrooms. Add the onions and cook, stirring occasionally, until soft. Stir in the garlic, tomatoes, wine, parsley, 1 teaspoon salt, basil, oregano, nutmeg, and thyme. Bring the mixture to boiling, lower the heat, and cover; simmer for 20 minutes. Uncover the pot and cook, stirring occasionally, until the sauce is thick, about 30 minutes. Remove from the heat.

While the vegetables and sauce are cooking, sprinkle the zucchini with the remaining teaspoon of salt. Let stand for 30 minutes; pat dry. Add the zucchini to the sauce.

Cook the lasagna noodles in boiling salted water following the package directions. Drain, rinse with cold water, and drain again.

Preheat the oven to 350°F.

To assemble, spread about a third of the tomato sauce in a 9- by 13- by 2-inch baking dish; top with a third of the lasagna, then ⅔ cup of the ricotta cheese and 1 cup Monterey Jack. Repeat the layers twice, ending with the cheeses. Sprinkle Parmesan cheese and almonds over the top. Bake, uncovered, in the oven for 50 minutes or until the center is heated through and the almonds are lightly browned. Remove from the oven and let stand for 20 minutes. Sprinkle with olives and cut into squares to serve.

Granny and Papa were always so glad when people stopped by; even unannounced, they didn't mind. Granny always had coffee and cookies or some treat to offer.

All week, Granny and Papa looked forward to Sunday, when they hoped the house would be full of people. The commotion of people and dogs did not bother them; the more the merrier. If not many people showed up, Granny and Papa got kind of sad. Granny would cook supper for all who were able to make it. Sometimes she wouldn't know how many people would show up, but she always had enough food for everyone. And it was always good!

Original painting of Granny and Papa's garden by Tilli Calhoun

Now that I live in their house on Mines Road, I try to keep a good supply of food in the cupboards or freezer. You never know who will show up.

We have kept up the tradition of getting the family together on Christmas Eve and Easter, since our house can hold everyone. We are happy to get together and continue the tradition that Granny and Papa began.

My husband, Warren, has also kept up Papa's tradition of growing red onions. He even gets some really big ones like Papa used to raise.

I remember going on cattle roundups with Papa. We would have to get up around 5:30 a.m. He would already be up and have his cowboy coffee brewing and bacon and eggs frying. This was the only time I saw Papa cooking. The coffee had grounds in it, the bacon wasn't cooked all the way, and the eggs still had the clear part runny. They tasted good anyway. After breakfast, we had to go out in the dark to catch and saddle our horses. We thought we were a big help. Luckily, Papa also had real cowboys helping him. When we were done for the day, we came back to the house and Granny would have a good hot lunch for everyone.

When we were kids, Granny and Papa had grandchildren staying with them almost every weekend. It was usually a bunch of us, not just one or two. All weekend long, we would go hiking or horseback riding. Our day-long adventures would take us to the lookout or down to the creek. Because we did a lot of things with our cousins, we are close like brothers and sisters. Even now, we all keep in touch and are interested in what everyone is doing. I'm glad Granny kept us all together.

—Wendy Howe

Green Spaghetti

I chose this recipe because it was a favorite at the home of my maternal grandparents, Louis and Elsie Madsen. Gramma was Italian, but my Danish Papa would be the one fixing it.

KIM BONDE

1 pound spaghetti, freshly cooked, drained, and still very hot
1 head garlic, separated into cloves
1 large bunch fresh basil, stems removed, leaves finely chopped
1 cup freshly grated Parmesan cheese
4 tablespoons butter, cut into small pieces
½ cup olive oil
Salt

Using a garlic press, press the cloves into the pot of hot spaghetti. Add the basil, cheese, and butter and toss gently. Add the olive oil and salt to taste and toss again.
Serve immediately!

The Madsen's twenty-fifth wedding anniversary, 1961
Standing: Roma Madsen, Hans Bonde, Bobby Frick, Ruth Frick
Sitting: Debbie Rasmussen, Aaron Rasmussen, Ione Holm

Louis and Elsie Madsen celebrating their twenty-fifth anniversary, 1961

Granny's Spaghetti

Makes about 7 cups

Granny made her spaghetti sauce in her pressure cooker, using her own canned or stewed tomatoes. Most of us are afraid of pressure cookers and don't have the time to can our own tomatoes, so we adjusted her recipe slightly to work for us.

IONE TEETER HOLM

The Holm cousins and their dogs
Standing: Gary Holm, Brett Holm,
Dave Holm with Dingo, Chad South,
Merry Calhoun, Warren Howe,
Cheryl and Jim Holm
Sitting: Susie Calhoun with Utah,
Nancy Calhoun with Honey, Peggy
Holm, Wendy Neely with Mindy, Lori
Neely South with Christy

1 (½-ounce) package dried porcini mushrooms (or other dried mushrooms)

1 cup hot water

2 tablespoons olive oil or salad oil

1 onion, chopped

2 stalks celery, chopped

1 clove garlic, minced

2 pounds ground beef

2 (14.5-ounce) cans stewed tomatoes

2 (6-ounce) cans tomato paste

1 tablespoon sugar

½ teaspoon Italian seasoning

1 bay leaf

Salt and pepper

1 pound spaghetti

Put the dried mushrooms in a small bowl and pour the hot water over them. Set aside. Heat the oil in a large skillet. Add the onion, celery, and garlic and sauté until tender, but not brown. Add the ground beef to the onions and garlic and brown; drain off the fat. Stir in the tomatoes, tomato paste, sugar, Italian seasoning, and bay leaf. Season with salt and pepper to taste. Drain the water from the mushrooms, cut them into thin slices, and add them to the sauce. Cover and simmer for 30 minutes. Remove the bay leaf and continue to simmer, covered, for 30 minutes. Remove the lid for the last 15 minutes.

When the sauce is almost done, cook the spaghetti, following the instructions on the package. Place the cooked spaghetti in a large, shallow bowl, pour the sauce over the top, and serve immediately.

Wendy Neely on Nyx, Dave
Holm on Sugar, Merry
Calhoun on Jamie

Macaroni, Tomato, and Cheese Casserole   *Serves 8*

This recipe is really good on a cold evening.

WENDY NEELY HOWE

1 (16-ounce) package rigatoni or rotelle pasta
1 pound ground beef
1 medium-size onion, finely chopped
1 large green bell pepper, finely chopped
½ teaspoon salt
2 (14.5-ounce) cans stewed tomatoes
8 ounces shredded Cheddar cheese (about 2 cups)

Preheat the oven to 350°F.

Fill a pot with water, bring to a boil, and cook the rigatoni according to the package directions; drain.

Meanwhile, in a 12-inch skillet over high heat, cook the ground beef, onion, and green pepper until all the pan juices evaporate and the meat is browned. Stir in the salt and tomatoes with their liquid; heat to boiling. Decrease the heat to low and simmer, uncovered, for 10 minutes, stirring occasionally. Add the drained pasta to the skillet and stir to combine.

Spoon the pasta mixture into a 9- by 13-inch baking dish or a 3-quart casserole and top with the shredded cheese. Loosely cover the dish with foil; do not let the foil touch the cheese. Bake for 20 minutes or until the mixture is hot and the cheese is melted.

Christmas 1992
Back: Warren and Wendy Howe,
Patsy and Hank Neely, Chad South
Front: Jessica South, Jamie South,
and Lori South

Granny, Wendy Neely
Howe, and Patsy Holm
Neely on Christmas Day

122

Grandma Ann Calhoun's Pizza

This was a summertime staple at our house when we were young. Neighborhood friends would come to swim and then have what we called "Pizza Things." I double the recipe sometimes because it keeps awhile. You can also add one teaspoon each of dried basil and minced garlic.

BECKY CALHOUN FOSTER

1 pound Velveeta cheese, softened
¾ cup (1½ sticks) margarine, softened
1 bunch chopped green onions (green and white parts)
1 tablespoon dried parsley
1½ tablespoon oregano
½ teaspoon salt
1 small can tomato paste
1 loaf French bread, cut into ½-inch slices

Preheat the oven to 350°F. In a bowl, blend together the Velveeta cheese and margarine. Add the onions, parsley, oregano, salt, and tomato paste. Spread the mixture on the slices. Bake in the oven for 8 minutes or until bubbling. You can also cook this under the broiler.

Camping in Montana
Standing in back: Becky Foster
Front: Ken, Reg and Susie
Calhoun, Harold Foster

The Calhoun Cousins

The Holm and Calhoun families both had ranches on Mines Road in Livermore. In May 1947, Tilli Holm went to visit Noel Johnson at the Calhoun ranch. When Tilli walked in, Noel and her cousin Wayne Calhoun were playing the piano and Wayne saw the woman he wanted to marry. Three years later, Wayne and Tilli did marry, and the two families began celebrating holidays together. Wayne's only brother, Ken, and his family would come to Livermore to celebrate Easter. The Wayne Calhoun family would travel to the Ken Calhoun family's home in Yuba City to celebrate Thanksgiving. The cousins looked forward to their holiday visits, which, with seven children in one house, could be quite exciting. Both families have an appreciation of the outdoors instilled in all by their father and grandfather, Reg. Be it photography, fishing, hunting, or hiking, the gatherings always include food. From venison to turkey, a grill is usually involved, along with a bottle of wine. Their fondness for nature led Ken and his wife, Vivian, to Hebgen Lake, Montana. After many summer vacations at a lodge, Ken and Vivian built their own summer home, where the Yuba City Calhouns have hosted the Livermore Calhouns. Trips to Yellowstone Park are a specialty—they know exactly where to find the bison and grizzly bears. I will never forget fly fishing on the Madison River, followed by dinner at The Grizzly Bar.

—Susie Calhoun

Veggie Pizzas

These pizzas can be made using any of your favorite veggies. This recipe uses some of mine. You can use Italian sausage or Canadian bacon for a topping, also. If you can't find the tomato-basil salad dressing, an Italian or goddess dressing will work, too.

BECKY CALHOUN FOSTER

1 tablespoon olive oil

2 cups of a combination of thinly sliced zucchini, mushrooms, tomatoes, and yellow onions

1 large Boboli pizza shell

¼ to ½ cup best-quality tomato basil salad dressing

1 cup shredded Cheddar cheese

Preheat the oven to 400°F.

In a small frying pan, heat the oil and sauté the vegetables until soft but not mushy. Arrange the mixture on top of the pizza shell. Top with the tomato-basil dressing, to taste, and the Cheddar cheese. Bake for 10 minutes, then place under broiler for 1 minute or until the cheese is bubbling. Serve immediately.

Portobello Pizzettas

Makes 12 servings

This was one of our favorites from our Italian dinner with our gourmet dining group. If you like portobello mushrooms, you will love these little pizzas.

BECKY CALHOUN FOSTER

5 ounces package frozen chopped spinach, thawed

1½ cups shredded mozzarella cheese

½ cup coarsely chopped pepperoni

1 teaspoon dried basil, crushed

¼ teaspoon coarsely ground black pepper

12 portobello mushrooms (3 to 4 inches in diameter), cleaned, stems removed

2 tablespoons margarine, melted

Fresh basil leaves (optional), as garnish

Preheat the oven to 350°F.

Press the liquid out of the spinach and finely chop. In a mixing bowl, combine the spinach, cheese, pepperoni, basil, and pepper. Place the mushrooms, open side up, on a lightly greased baking sheet and brush with margarine. Spoon 2 tablespoons of the cheese mixture into each mushroom.

Bake the mushrooms in the oven for 12 minutes or until heated through. An alternate cooking method is to place them on the unheated rack of a broiler pan and broil 4 inches from the heat for 3 to 4 minutes. If desired, garnish with fresh basil.

When I reflect back on my years at Route #1, Box 6, Livermore-Pleasanton Road, "Fair View," I think of hard work, good food, and family gatherings. Fair View was such a beautiful farm, with its big Victorian house, barns, tank house, silo, sheds, and coops. There were many trees—almond, orange, lemon, palm, pine, eucalyptus, a walnut orchard, and a huge pepper tree that we would climb and sit in.

The hub of the house was the large kitchen, with its big oval oak table covered with a blue-and-white checked oilcloth. It was warm and filled with great smells. There was nothing like the aroma of our mother's roasts, apple pies, and coffee.

On Sunday, Grandpa Teeter would come for dinner, bringing a copy of Life magazine and candy. We would race down the long sidewalk to greet him and help carry the "goodies." He sat in the big wooden armchair with the soft cushion, brushing off our cat, Mikey, who claimed the chair the rest of the week. Sunday dinner with all of the family was a tradition we carried on until our mother died.

Original drawing of Fair View by Tilli Calhoun

(back) Frank Teeter with Patsy in front, Tilli Holm, Verna Fachner Saxton (front) Frank Holm, Ione Teeter Holm with Jim Holm in front, Rich Holm

Holidays were always special. I remember Christmas Eve, with the long wooden tables that Grandpa Teeter had made stretching from the living room into the dining room. They were covered in white linen with tall red candles, fragrant greens, dishes of Christmas hard candies and homemade salted almonds and sugared walnuts from our orchard.

Our father had a huge vegetable garden. He grew the tallest corn and beans as well as tomatoes, peppers, and cucumbers—enough to can and share with friends and relatives. A special holiday treat was our mother's Danish pickles. Members of the Presbyterian Church would look forward to purchasing them at their annual bazaar.

Hank and I had our wedding reception in the big house. We lived there for three years in the apartment where my mother and father had started their married life. In 1960 we moved to a home we built on Mines Road.

Our summers were spent at the Circle H Ranch. There, Stockton red onions were grown and sold to Lou Gardella's Del Valle Mercantile. The Ranch's Hereford cattle were sold for meat and the Holsteins sold as milk cows. Their cream was taken to the railroad station in Livermore and sent to the Tomales Bay Creamery. When the horses weren't being used for work, we rode them over the hills. The long tables on the screened porch were always filled with relatives and friends. A special Sunday treat was if somebody brought up ice from town; we could make home-churned strawberry or peach ice cream.

During deer season, there was always a big barbecue. The venison was marinated in Jesse Rasmussen's famous sauce. Everyone brought special dishes, and there were lots of tubs of beer and soda. What a joy it was to get a nickel to buy an orange soda. There was much to do—swimming, playing cards, horseshoes, dancing, and much talking and eating. What a life!

The 1906 Earthquake

In April of 1906, Carl and Ida Holm were attending a Danish convention in San Francisco and staying at the Winchester Hotel. At 5:12 a.m. on Wednesday, April 18, the magnitude 7.9 earthquake struck. Carl was awakened by the shock and went to the windows from which he could see up and down Third Street. Just as he reached the window the front of a two-story brick building across the street toppled over, filling the street with debris. Two other buildings collapsed at the same instant, blocking the streets and sidewalks and filling the air with suffocating dust. Carl and Ida quickly dressed. As they made their way out, they checked on a neighbor, only to find him crushed by a chimney in his hotel room. They passed over several dead bodies on their way to the street. Continuing on foot toward the hills in the northern part of San Francisco, they witnessed the great city being swept away by fire. Carl and Ida traveled to the waterfront, crossing over sunken ground, to catch a ferry shuttling refugees to Oakland. It took them three days to return to Livermore. With no working telephones or telegraphs, the family was worried they may have perished in the earthquake.

Dick Holm recalled feeling the earthquake in Livermore. Only five years old at the time, he thought his brothers, Art and Leslie—known for their practical jokes—were playing a trick on him. Lou Gardella, a family friend, said that as a child, he had gone up to a hilltop on the north side of Livermore to see the flames as San Francisco burned. The water tank and chimney at the Livermore railroad depot collapsed. Local drugstores reported hundreds of dollars worth of merchandise had been knocked to the floor.

126

Rice, Beans, Casseroles, and Other Dishes

Frank Teeter, Ione Teeter, Hattie Puntney Teeter, 1907

Frank Teeter
(Ione's father)

Daniel and Carolyn Arnett
Teeter (Ione's grandparents)

Reba, Gray, Ione, and Ed Teeter

The Teeter men:
Daniel, Thurman, Desmond, and
Frank holding Gray

Ed Teeter and
friends

Ed Teeter on the hood of
the Cresta Blanca truck

Carl Stebbins,
Frank Holm,
Gray Teeter, and
Jim Holm with
"The Lincoln"

Reba Teeter Kilgo,
Bill Kilgo, Dick Holm
holding Frank Holm, Flora Teeter, Frank
Teeter holding Tilli Holm

Tamale Pie

Serves 8

One of the favorite dishes served in the school cafeteria at the Fifth Street School in the late 1930s and '40s was the tamale pie. This recipe came from my mother-in-law, Billie Chrysostomo Calhoun.

MERILYN "TILLI" HOLM CALHOUN

2 tablespoons olive oil
2 large onions, diced
1 clove garlic, minced
1 bell pepper, seeds and veins removed, diced, or 1 (4-ounce) can chopped green chilies
1½ pounds ground beef (about 3 cups)
1 (14.5-ounce) can whole tomatoes
1 (15.25-ounce) can whole-kernel corn
1 (6-ounce) can small black olives
1 cup cornmeal
1 (8-ounce) can tomato sauce
1 tablespoon Worcestershire sauce
2 teaspoons chili powder
Salt and pepper
¾ cup milk

Preheat the oven to 350°F and oil a 4-quart casserole. In a large skillet over medium heat, add the olive oil. Add the onions, garlic, pepper, and beef, and brown. Mix in the tomatoes, corn, olives, cornmeal, tomato sauce, Worcestershire sauce, chili powder, salt, pepper, and milk. Transfer the mixture to the casserole and bake for 45 minutes or until bubbling.

Original sketches of the Livermore Public School and the Fifth Street School by Tilli Calhoun, drawn for the anniversary program

Roundup crew: Tony George, Wayne Calhoun, Les Holm, Dick "Papa" Holm with Gary Holm, Rich Holm

Granny's Cowboy Beans

Serves 8

Roundups to brand cattle took place at the Circle H Ranch on Mines Road since the 1920s. A traditional dish served to the hungry cowboys by Ione Holm was her cowboy beans, along with French bread, a green salad, and her famous huge chocolate cake.

IONE TEETER HOLM

1½ pounds ground beef
1 bell pepper, diced
1 large onion, diced
2 or 3 stalks celery, diced
2 (28-ounce) cans kidney beans
1 quart stewed tomatoes
1 teaspoon salt
¼ teaspoon pepper
Dash chili powder (optional)

In a large skillet over medium heat, brown the beef, bell pepper, onion, and celery. Transfer the beef and sautéed vegetables into a large pot. Add the kidney beans and tomatoes, and season to taste with salt, pepper, and chili powder. Simmer for 2 to 3 hours or until the beans are cooked and the flavors have melded.

Chili con Carne

This recipe from Pat Teel has become fondly known as "Teel's Chili" among my friends. Lou Ann McCune has adapted it over the years; she will barbecue a small tri-tip, cut it into ½-inch strips, and add it with the other meats for barbecue flavoring. This chili is well known for its volatility and is best enjoyed among really good friends and forgiving family in the great outdoors.

SUSIE CALHOUN from Pat Teel

4 cups beans (kidney, pink, or pinto)

4 quarts meat stock

1 pound bacon, cut into ½-inch dice

1 cup chopped fresh parsley

½ cup chopped bell pepper

4 fresh jalapeño peppers or hot chilies
    of your choice (optional)

1 chopped onion

10 cloves garlic, minced

1 cup sliced fresh white mushrooms

2 pounds ground beef

2 (15-ounce) cans Mexican-flavored
    stewed tomatoes

2 (12-ounce) cans tomato paste

1 (7.75-ounce) can El Pato tomato sauce

1 tablespoon chili powder

1 tablespoon dried oregano

1 teaspoon ground coriander

1 teaspoon cumin

4 teaspoons salt

In a large nonreactive pot or bowl, soak the beans overnight. In the morning, drain the beans and put them in a large pot. Add the meat stock and cook for 2 hours. In a skillet, sauté the bacon, parsley, bell pepper, peppers, onion, garlic, and mushrooms until soft; add them to the beans. In the same skillet, brown the meat; then add it and the drippings to the beans. Stir in the tomatoes, tomato paste, sauce, chili powder, oregano, and coriander. Season to taste with cumin and salt. Simmer another hour until the beans are tender and the flavors are melded.

Jane Drummond, Craig Teel, Susie Calhoun, and Lou Ann McCune, 1974

Black Bean Enchiladas

CARLA STEBBINS CANTER

1 (16-ounce) package dried black beans

1 tablespoon chili powder

1 teaspoon ground cumin seed

1 (28-ounce) can Las Palmas mild
  enchilada sauce

1 dozen fresh corn tortillas

1 medium onion, finely diced

1 to 2 cups shredded Monterey Jack
  cheese

1 bunch fresh cilantro

16 ounces fat-free sour cream

Tina Stebbins, Gladys Benthien,
Jon and Carla Stebbins

Soak the beans overnight, then drain and discard the water they were soaked in.

Cook the beans according to the directions on the package. As the beans are cooking, add the chili powder and cumin. When the beans are done, heat the enchilada sauce over medium heat for approximately 5 to 10 minutes.

Preheat the oven to 375°F and oil a 9- by 13-inch baking dish.

While the sauce is heating, warm the tortillas. Either coat a skillet lightly with vegetable oil and lightly fry them, or, for a crisp tortilla, warm them in a skillet with or without nonstick spray. Either method is fine, as long as the tortillas becomes crisp and are no longer soft.

Immediately after "crisping" the tortillas, use tongs to dip each one into the hot enchilada sauce. Cover the tortilla completely with the sauce. Carefully remove the tortilla and place it flat on a dinner plate. On one half of the dipped tortilla, place about 2 tablespoons of the bean mixture, a pinch of onions, and a pinch of grated cheese. Roll the tortilla, beginning on the side with the mixture. Place the rolled tortilla in the baking dish.

Repeat the process with each tortilla. Place only 1 layer in the baking dish; do not stack. Pour the remaining sauce over the enchiladas and top with the remaining cheese and onions. Bake for 35 to 45 minutes, or until the sauce is bubbling and the cheese melted. Garnish each serving with a dollop of sour cream and a pinch of the fresh cilantro. You could also pass the sour cream and cilantro at the table.

Tortilla-Bean Casserole

Makes 10 to 12 side-dish servings or 6 to 8 main-dish servings

IRIS MURRAY STEBBINS

2 cups chopped onion

1½ cups chopped green bell pepper

1 (14.5-ounce) can diced tomatoes, with
their juices

¾ cup picante sauce

2 cloves garlic, minced

2 teaspoons ground cumin

2 (15-ounce) cans black beans or
kidney beans, drained

12 (6-inch) corn tortillas

2 cups shredded low-fat Monterey Jack
cheese (about 8 ounces)

2 medium tomatoes, sliced (optional)

2 cups shredded lettuce (optional)

Sliced green onion (optional)

½ cup low-fat sour cream or plain yogurt
(optional)

Sliced pitted olives (optional)

Preheat the oven to 350°F. In a large skillet over high heat, combine the onion, green pepper, tomatoes and juice, picante sauce, garlic, and cumin. Bring the mixture to a boil, then reduce the heat and simmer, uncovered, for 10 minutes. Stir in the beans.

Spread a third of the bean mixture on the bottom of a 9- by 13- by 2-inch baking dish. Cover with half of the tortillas, overlapping as necessary, and half of the cheese. Add another third of the bean mixture, then the remaining tortillas, and the last of the bean mixture. Cover the dish with foil and bake for 30 to 35 minutes, or until heated through. Sprinkle with the remaining cheese and let stand for 10 minutes.

After baking, you can top the casserole with tomato slices, lettuce, green onion, and olives. Cut into squares to serve. If desired, top with sour cream or yogurt.

Iris Murray Stebbins in center, with friends at the Pacific Ocean, 1944.

Wild Rice with Mushrooms

This rice dish goes nicely with any duck dinner. The recipe came from a friend of my mother. You can make this a day ahead and refrigerate.

CINDY CALHOUN MILLER

1 cup raw wild rice, washed well, drained

1 teaspoon salt

3 cups water

2 tablespoons butter

½ pound fresh mushrooms, sliced

6 strips bacon, finely chopped

1 medium-size onion, chopped

1 cup finely chopped celery

½ cup tomato juice, plus more as needed

In a pot over low heat, combine the rice, salt, and water. Simmer for 35 to 45 minutes or until the rice is tender. Drain.

Preheat the oven to 350°F. In a skillet over medium-high heat, melt the butter, then add the mushrooms and sauté until soft. Put the mushrooms in a small bowl and set aside. In the same skillet, sauté the bacon, celery, and onions until the vegetables are limp. Pour off any extra bacon fat. Combine the mushrooms, vegetables, tomato juice, and rice. Pour into a casserole and bake for about 30 minutes.

Remembering Ione

One of my favorite memories of Granny was when we would go to the Heifer Carnival at the First Presbyterian Church in Livermore each year. As always, we went up to the hills to Granny's house on the weekend of the carnival. After putting on our costumes (the most memorable was the year that my sister dressed up as a pig), we would all drive downtown. The moment we walked in the door, everyone would come up to greet Granny. She was a very popular attendee. The Heifer Carnival had games, food, and a haunted house. But in my opinion, the best was the cakewalk. For many years, Granny would make a chocolate cake, cover it with homemade whipped cream (Richie's favorite), and donate it to the cakewalk. My sister and I tried numerous times to win her cake.

When I was younger, we would spend weekends with Granny and help around the house. Some nights we would sit in her chair with her and watch Wheel of Fortune *and* Jeopardy. *Almost every Sunday, we would have dinner at Granny's along with other family members. Our dinners usually consisted of vegetables from Papa's garden and a roast or baked chicken. (After Papa died, the vegetables came from Richie's garden.) If we were lucky, Granny would have purchased bonbon ice cream treats for dessert. At the table, there were unspoken seat assignments which everyone abided by. I would usually sit in Richie's seat on the weekends he was not with us in the hills. When Richie was there, Granny would let me sit right next to her, at the head of the table. It made me feel very special to sit right next to her while we ate dinner.*

— *Jamie South, great-granddaughter*

Asparagus Fried Rice

Serves 8

SANDY SPORTS HOLM

2 cups uncooked white rice

Soy sauce

Oil

2 eggs, beaten

1 large bunch asparagus, cut diagonally into 1-inch pieces

5 green onions, chopped

1 small yellow onion, diced

1 (8-ounce) can sliced water chestnuts

Cook the rice according to the instructions on the package. When it is cooked, add soy sauce to taste and mix well.

In a wok or heavy skillet, add a small amount of oil and scramble the eggs. Set aside.

If needed, add a little more oil to the wok, then add the asparagus and stir-fry until bright green and slightly crunchy, about 1 to 2 minutes. Add the asparagus to the rice. Add the green onions to the wok and stir-fry until bright green and slightly crunchy, about 1 to 2 minutes. Add the green onions to the rice. Add the yellow onion to the wok and stir-fry until translucent, about 1 to 2 minutes, then add it to the rice. Stir-fry the water chestnuts until warmed through, then add them to the rice. Chop the scrambled egg into small pieces and add them to the rice. Mix together and serve.

Mario and Kelly Garcia's Wedding at the Circle H Ranch, June 18, 2005 Left to right: Dave and Sandy Sports Holm, Frank and Joan Holm, Mario and Kelly Garcia, Carla and Marcos Garcia, Jennifer Holm

Les and Lois Holm

Rice Parisienne

I serve this with a Caesar salad and add crumbled Gorgonzola cheese to the rice just before serving. Garlic bread is a nice addition, too. In place of the canned mushrooms in this recipe, I often use fresh mushrooms, which I slice and sauté until lightly browned, and then add to the cooked rice. As an alternative to stove-top cooking, you can finish this dish in the oven. Just transfer the rice and vegetable mixture to a buttered casserole, cover, and cook about an hour at 325°F, stirring occasionally.

LOIS HANSEN HOLM

2 tablespoons butter or margarine
1 cup uncooked rice
2 (7-ounce) cans mushroom stems and pieces, drained
2 (14-ounce) cans chicken broth
1 (1.1-ounce) envelope onion soup mix
¼ cup sherry
2 tablespoons chopped fresh parsley
1 teaspoon garlic powder

In a heavy frying pan (cast iron, if you have it) over medium heat, melt the butter. Add the rice and cook, stirring, until golden. Add the mushrooms, broth, soup mix, sherry, parsley, and garlic powder, and stir to mix.

Decrease the heat to low, cover the pan tightly (use aluminum foil if you don't have a tight-fitting lid), and cook for about 30 minutes. Stir occasionally, scraping the bottom of the pan so the rice doesn't stick.

Let the dish sit uncovered for about 10 minutes before serving.

Left to right: Bob Holm, grandmother Mona Holm holding Staci Holm, and grandfather Les Holm holding Bryan Holm

The Cherubs with Papa and Granny waiting for the California Zephyr.
Back: Papa holding Jimmy Holm, Gary Holm, Granny holding Nancy Calhoun.
Front: David Holm, Susie Calhoun (with pigtails), Lori and Wendy Keely, Peggy
Holm, Merry Calhoun. Pleasanton, May 26, 1962

Dick and Ione Holm's grandchildren and great-grandchildren

All of the grandchildren spent a lot of time with Dick and Ione. To this day, the cousins enjoy each other's company and spend a lot of time together.

Brett, Jennifer, and Derek Holm

Back: Jamie South, Clint Gibson, Stacey Holm Front: Jennifer Holm, Jessica South, Marcos Garcia, 2007

Our first Piñata Easter on the Calhoun's flats, 1966

Great-grandchildren waiting for Santa to arrive: Jamie South, Jessica South, Stacey Holm, Jennifer Holm, Colin Rennick, Carla Garcia, Mario Garcia Standing: Whitney Carter, Molly Rennick, Laina Carter

Derek, Eihdel, and Charlene Holm, 2006

The Holm cousins, 1998
Back: Nancy, Merry, Wendy, Lori, Peggy, Susie Front: David, Gary, Jim

Sweet and Sour Zucchini

Serves 10

These tasty zukes keep well in the refrigerator for weeks.

JOAN AND FRANK HOLM

2 tablespoons dehydrated onions

2 tablespoons apple cider vinegar

¾ cup sugar

1 teaspoon salt

½ teaspoon pepper

½ cup salad oil

⅔ cup red wine vinegar

½ cup chopped green bell pepper

½ cup chopped celery

5 uncooked zucchini (each about 7 inches
   long), very thinly sliced

Place the onions in a small bowl and add the cider vinegar. Let them stand for 30 minutes. Then whisk in the sugar, salt, pepper, oil, and vinegar.

In a large bowl, combine the bell pepper, celery, and zucchini. Pour the vinegar-onion mixture over the vegetables and blend well. Marinate in the refrigerator overnight or for at least 6 hours. Drain and serve cold.

Brunede Kartofler (Sugar-Browned Potatoes) *Serves 4*

Grandma Ida Holm, the daughter of Danish immigrants, became known as one of Livermore's better cooks. In 1918 she was asked to oversee food preparation for a rodeo. This fundraiser for the Red Cross began Livermore's tradition of an annual rodeo. Grandma Holm's kitchen always hummed with activity on Christmas Eve as dinner was served to forty or so family members. This is one of my favorite recipes of Ida's—a traditional Danish dish of caramelized potatoes that she served with green kale.

MERILYN "TILLI" HOLM CALHOUN

2 pounds small new potatoes

2 tablespoons sugar

4 tablespoons butter

Cook the potatoes in boiling salted water until tender, about 10 minutes. Drain. When they are cool enough to handle, peel and slice them; rinse them in cold water. In a frying pan, melt the sugar over low heat, stirring continuously until it is golden brown in color. Stir in the butter until well blended. Add the potatoes to the sugar and butter, shaking the pan gently until the potatoes are evenly glazed and golden brown. Serve warm.

Roasted Potatoes with Onions

Serves 4

WENDY NEELY HOWE

1 (1-ounce) envelope onion soup mix

2 pounds baking potatoes, cut into large
    chunks

⅓ cup olive or vegetable oil

Preheat the oven to 450°F.

In large plastic bag or bowl, combine the soup mix, potatoes and oil. Close the bag and shake, or toss together in the bowl, until the potatoes are evenly coated. Spread the potatoes evenly in a 9- by 13-inch baking dish. Bake, uncovered, stirring occasionally, for 40 minutes, or until the potatoes are tender and golden brown.

Yams with Fresh Orange Sauce

Serves 12

I was never a fan of yams until I found this recipe at Thanksgiving one year. I come from a long line of yam-eaters who all wanted this recipe.

JANET FACHNER VON TOUSSAINT

6 medium purple yams

2 tablespoons melted butter plus more
    for oiling the pan

1 cup freshly squeezed orange juice

1 tablespoon cornstarch

¼ cup packed brown sugar

¼ cup granulated sugar

Zest of ½ orange, finely grated

2 tablespoons light Karo corn syrup

⅛ teaspoon grated nutmeg

⅛ teaspoon ground cinnamon

½ cup pecans, chopped

1 red apple, cored and sliced

1 green apple, cored and sliced

Place the yams in a pot and cover with water. Bring to a boil, then decrease the heat to a simmer and cook until tender. When cool enough to handle, peel and slice.

Preheat the oven to 350°F and butter a 9- by 13-inch baking dish. In a saucepan over medium heat, combine the butter, juice, cornstarch, sugars, zest, corn syrup, nutmeg, and cinnamon. Heat until the sauce thickens, stirring constantly.

Make alternating layers of yam slices, pecans, and apple slices in the baking dish. Pour the sauce over the layers and bake for 45 minutes, or until the apples are cooked and the sauce is bubbling.

Potato Casserole

Serves 8

VELMA CARTER

¼ cup (½ stick) melted butter or margarine
  plus more for buttering the dish
1 (1-pound) package frozen hash brown
  potatoes, defrosted
½ cup cream of chicken soup
1 cup shredded sharp Cheddar cheese
¼ cup chopped onion
¼ teaspoon salt
1 cup sour cream
1 cup crushed cornflakes

Preheat the oven to 350°F and butter a 9- by 13-inch casserole dish. In a large bowl, combine the butter, potatoes, soup, cheese, onion, salt, and sour cream. Mix well. Transfer to the casserole and top with the crushed cornflakes. Bake for 45 minutes or until the potatoes are heated through and the cornflakes are lightly browned.

Sweet Potato and Apple Bake

Serves 8

MERILYN "TILLI" HOLM CALHOUN

6 tablespoons butter, cut into small pieces
  plus more for buttering the dish
1 pound sweet potatoes, peeled and sliced
1 pound green apples, peeled, cored,
  and sliced
1 teaspoon salt
½ cup brown sugar
1 teaspoon grated nutmeg
1 tablespoon freshly squeezed lemon juice

Preheat the oven to 400°F, and butter a 9- by 13-inch casserole dish.

Layer the sweet potatoes and apples in the casserole. Sprinkle each layer with salt, sugar, nutmeg, and lemon juice; dot with butter. Bake for 40 minutes. After 20 minutes, stir the apples and potatoes to keep the top layer moist. Turn the oven up to 450°F for the last 10 minutes to caramelize the sugars. The dish is done when the potatoes and apples are cooked through and the juices are bubbling.

Tilli Calhoun painting at the Arts Festival at Carnegie Park in Livermore, 1981. Standing: cousin Janet Fachner, Bob Moore, and Clay Dickens with friend

Tater Tot Casserole

For this dish, Lloyd would use whatever fresh vegetables were in his garden. You can use a package of frozen vegetables if you don't have garden-fresh at hand.

LLOYD MARSH

Vegetable oil spray for oiling the dish
1 pound ground beef
1 onion, diced
Vegetables, approximately 8 cups fresh or 2 (16-ounce) bags frozen
1 (10.75-ounce) can cream of mushroom soup, undiluted
¾ cup water
1 (32-ounce) bag frozen Tater Tots
1 to 2 cups of shredded Cheddar and mozzarella cheese

Preheat the oven to 350°F. Spray a 9- by 13-inch casserole dish with cooking spray.

In a frying pan over medium heat, add the ground beef and onion. Sauté until brown, and drain off the fat. In a pot fitted with a steaming rack, steam the vegetables until tender. In a small saucepan over medium heat, combine the soup and water. Stir until heated and well blended. Alternate layers of the beef mixture and the vegetables in the casserole dish. Pour the soup over the top layer. Cover neatly with a layer of Tater Tots and finish with the cheese. Bake for 45 to 60 minutes or until the cheese is melted.

Ruth Marsh, Blanche George,
Sandy Sanders

Meat, Fish, and Poultry

Circle H Ranch, circa 1930

HOLM BROS

The Ranch

In 1926, Leslie and Dick Holm purchased a ranch on Mines Road in the Livermore hills from Charles and Mathilda Detjens Graham, relatives of Mona Detjens Holm. This first parcel became the Circle H Ranch, where Leslie and Dick raised cattle until they died. Throughout the years, parcels were purchased, increasing the size to sixteen hundred acres, stretching from the Arroyo Mocho Creek up and over Crane Ridge. The ranch is currently managed by Leslie and Dick's children and grandchildren.

There was a small cabin on the property, plus a Hetch Hetchy line shack, some sheds, and a barn. The shack has been remodeled throughout the years, with a variety of caretakers residing there: Chet Rasmussen, Ben Benthien, Blanche and Tony George, Tina Stebbins Barbera and Gina, Guy, and Joe Barbera, Susie Calhoun, Nancy and Bob Mueller, Lou Ann McCune, and Lowell Lull. In 1938, a water reservoir was added and is still used as a swimming pool today (the cement pond).

The Ranch had many visitors. In the summer, Dick and Ione would bring their kids, bedding, food, and a milk cow up in a cattle truck. The family would clear rocks from the fields, work on the springs, and fix fences. Spring was the time for the roundup; the family would gather the cattle from surrounding parcels for branding. During deer season, hunters would stay at the cabin to get in their morning and evening

Barbecuing at the Circle H Ranch Jim Holm, Russ Rasmussen, Wayne Calhoun, and Jesse Rasmussen

Original painting of July Fourth at the Circle H Ranch by Tilli Calhoun

Building the swimming pool at the Circle H Ranch, 1938

hunts. Originally, the benches and long picnic tables came from Camp Parks in Dublin.

The Circle H Ranch has also been the locale for many gatherings. Fourth of July is a potluck family reunion. Highlights would be a softball game, swimming, and homemade fireworks. In mid-August, the family hosted the annual deer barbecue, with venison from the ranch. Throughout the generations, there have been countless barbecues, weddings, and momentous birthday parties among the many memorable times.

Creamed Chicken

Serves 6 to 8

You can serve this chicken over rice or noodles. Biscuits or puff pastry are also quite tasty.

IONE TEETER HOLM

1 (5-pound) chicken
2 carrots, sliced
2 celery stalks, sliced
1 onion, sliced into thin rings
5 peppercorns
3 sprigs fresh parsley, chopped
4 tablespoons (½ stick) butter
1 pound fresh mushrooms, thinly sliced
⅓ cup flour
1 cup heavy cream
Pinch of poultry seasoning (if desired)

Place the chicken, carrots, celery, onion, peppercorns, and parsley in a large pot and cover with water. Bring to a boil, decrease the heat, and simmer for 1½ hours, or until the chicken is tender. Remove the chicken and continue to simmer the vegetables and stock for another hour. The liquid will reduce a bit. Meanwhile, remove the chicken meat from the bones and cut it into large pieces. Set aside. Strain the vegetables from the stock, and set the stock aside. Discard the vegetables.

In a frying pan over medium heat, melt the butter. Add the mushrooms and sauté until lightly browned. Sprinkle the mushrooms with flour and stir. Add 2 cups of the stock and the cream. Cook for about 5 minutes or until the liquids begin to thicken. Stir frequently. Add the chicken and the poultry seasoning and cook until the sauce has thickened and the chicken pieces are heated through.

Viva La Chicken

Serves 8

My mother-in-law, Bonnie Howe, gave this recipe to me. You can also substitute turkey leftover from Thanksgiving for the chicken.

WENDY NEELY HOWE

3 to 4 cups cooked shredded chicken
1 (10.5-ounce) can cream of chicken soup
1 (10.5-ounce) can cream of mushroom soup
⅔ cup milk
1 chopped onion
⅔ cup salsa
1 dozen corn tortillas
½ to 1 pound shredded Cheddar cheese

Preheat the oven to 300°F.

In a bowl, combine the chicken, soup, milk, onion, and salsa. Line the bottom of a 9- by 13-inch baking dish with 6 tortillas. Evenly spread the chicken mixture on top. Cover with 6 tortillas and sprinkle the cheese on top. Place in the oven and bake for 1 hour, or until bubbling.

Wayne's Barbecued Chicken

Serves 25 to 30

WAYNE CALHOUN

5 or 6 whole chickens (3½ to 4 pounds each)
Garlic salt
Lemon pepper
2 onions, chopped
5 cloves garlic, chopped
2 stalks celery, chopped
4 fresh rosemary sprigs
2 to 3 cups white wine, plus more if needed

Prepare the fire in a kettle-style barbecue or gas grill. Cut the chickens in half lengthwise. Sprinkle generously with garlic salt and lemon pepper. Place them on the barbecue and cook until almost done, about 15 minutes per side. They should still be pink in the middle. Remove from the grill and cut each half into 4 pieces. In a large pot with a rack, layer the chicken pieces with the onions, garlic, celery, and rosemary. Pour in the white wine. Cover, and place the pot on a burner over low heat, and steam for 30 to 40 minutes. Check occasionally to make sure all the wine hasn't evaporated, adding more if needed. The chicken is done when the juices run clear from a pierced thigh.

Wayne and Ken Calhoun barbecuing chicken at the Circle H with Honey, the biting dog.

Chinese Chicken

Serves 12

This recipe has always been a favorite. My mother, Phyllis Jorgensen Fachner, got this recipe from Ida Murray, Iris Stebbins' mother. She serves it with a molded Jell-o salad and dinner rolls at special ladies' luncheons for the family. We still laugh at the story of one cook (she will remain nameless) who substituted the wet kind of chow mein noodles and wondered why the dish was so soggy.

JANET FACHNER VON TOUSSAINT

1 large (3 to 4 pound) chicken
2 (15-ounce) cans cream of mushroom soup
1 cup chicken broth
2 cups chopped celery
½ cup chopped green onion
1 (6-ounce) package whole roasted cashews (about 1¼ cups), reserving 2 ounces for garnish
1 (24-ounce) can crisp chow mein noodles, reserve about ¼ cup for garnish
Salt and pepper

Place the chicken in a large pot over high heat, cover with water and bring to a boil. Reduce the heat and simmer until the chicken is cooked, about 1 hour. Drain and let cool until easily handled. Remove the meat from the bones and cut into 1-inch pieces.

Preheat the oven to 350°F.

In a large bowl, combine the chicken, soup, broth, celery, onion, cashews, and noodles. Season with salt and pepper to taste and mix well. Spread in a 9- by 13-inch pan and bake for 40 minutes. Garnish with remaining cashews and noodles.

Chicken with Capers

Serves 4

MERRY "LAMBIE" CALHOUN CARTER

4 skinless, boneless chicken breasts, pounded to ¼ inch thick
1 tablespoon powdered instant chicken bouillon
2 tablespoons olive oil
⅓ pound fresh mushrooms, sliced (about 3 cups)
3 tablespoons capers
½ cup white wine

Rub the chicken with the bouillon powder. Heat the oil in a large skillet over medium-high heat. Sauté the chicken on both sides until golden brown. Remove to a warm serving platter. In the same pan, sauté the mushrooms until lightly browned. Cover the chicken with the mushrooms. Add the wine to the skillet, bring to a boil, and reduce the wine by half. Add the capers, keeping the skillet over the heat just long enough to heat them through. Pour the reduced wine-caper mixture over the chicken.

Oven Chicken

This is a great Sunday-dinner kind of meal that you can serve anytime. It's a real family favorite—served with rice or a baked potato, a vegetable, and a crispy green salad. Sometimes when I make this recipe, I dust the chicken pieces with Bisquick before baking them. You can also brown the chicken in a frying pan before baking it in the oven.

MARY FOXWORTHY RASMUSSEN

1 (3 to 4-pound) chicken, cut into pieces
2 cups buttermilk
Vegetable oil for oiling the dish
1 teaspoon salt
1 teaspoon pepper
¼ cup soy sauce
2 tablespoons honey
½ cup orange juice
1 (8-ounce) jar apricot jam

Place the chicken pieces in a plastic bag, add the buttermilk, seal the bag, and refrigerate overnight.

The next day when you are ready to cook the chicken, preheat the oven to 350°F and oil a shallow baking dish with vegetable oil. Drain the chicken and discard the marinade. Place the pieces in the baking dish, sprinkle with salt and pepper, and bake for 30 minutes.

While the chicken is baking, combine the soy sauce, honey, orange juice, and jam in a small bowl. Mix well. Carefully pour this mixture over the chicken and bake for another 30 minutes, or until done.

Russ Rasmussen family, 1999
Standing: Zachary, Mark, Robin, Russ,
Jess, Heather, Sean, Nicole, Alyssa
Seated: Holly, Mary, Terri

Russ and Mary Rasmussen's
grandchildren
Cody and Clint Petersen, Alyssa,
Monica, Nicole, and
Zachary Rasmussen

Wendy's Lemon Chicken

Serves 6

This is a favorite of our dinner guests.

WENDY NEELY HOWE

¼ cup flour
½ teaspoon salt
⅛ teaspoon pepper
6 boneless, skinless chicken breasts, pounded to ⅛ inch thick
2 to 3 tablespoons butter or margarine, plus more if needed
1 cup water
1 cube or envelope chicken-flavored bouillon
2 small lemons

In a plastic bag, combine the flour, salt, and pepper. Place a few of the chicken pieces in the plastic bag and shake to coat. Repeat until all the chicken pieces are coated. Reserve the remaining flour mixture.

In a 12-inch skillet over medium-high heat, melt the butter. Cook 3 of the chicken pieces at a time. Brown the chicken lightly on both sides, adding more butter if necessary. Remove the chicken pieces to a plate and decrease the heat to low. Stir the reserved flour mixture into the drippings in the skillet; add the water, bouillon, and the juice of half a lemon, stirring to loosen any browned bits on the bottom of the pan. Thinly slice the remaining lemons. Return the chicken to the skillet and top each piece with lemon slices. Cover and simmer for 5 minutes or until the chicken is fork-tender. To serve, arrange the chicken and lemon slices on a warm platter and pour the remaining sauce over the chicken.

Wendy Neely and
Merry Calhoun, 1959
Giddy-up, cowgirls!

Urban Chicken Pie

My family's farm, Fair View, was located between Stanley Boulevard and Alden Lane, west of Livermore. They farmed, ranched, and grew grapes from the late 1800s through the 1960s. My great-grandmother, Ida Jessen Holm, fed the family along with the farm and ranch-hands, neighbors, and the occasional hobo who hopped the Southern Pacific just north of the farm. One of her menus included a chicken pie she baked in a huge milk pan, using whole chicken pieces. I don't raise chickens or feed the crowds as she did, so this is my urban version.

NANCY CALHOUN MUELLER

Flaky pastry

1¼ cups unsifted flour

¼ teaspoon salt

3 tablespoons butter

3 tablespoons shortening

1 egg, separated, white reserved

2 tablespoons cold water

Filling

1 (5 to 6 pound) whole chicken, boiled

2 tablespoons olive oil

1 onion, finely chopped

2 stalks celery, finely chopped

2 cups mushrooms, sliced

3 tablespoons flour

Dash of white pepper

Dash of grated nutmeg

1½ cups chicken broth

½ cup Sauvignon Blanc

3 medium cooked carrots, sliced
    (cooked in the pot with the chicken)

1 cup frozen peas, thawed

Salt

To make the pastry, combine the flour and salt in a bowl. Using a pastry blender or two knives, cut in the butter and shortening until the mixture resembles coarse crumbs. In a small bowl, beat together the egg yolk and cold water; add to the flour mixture and stir with a fork until the pastry begins to hold together. You may need to add a bit more water. Shape the dough into a smooth ball, wrap well in plastic wrap, and refrigerate.

Preheat the oven to 425°F. Remove the chicken meat from the bones, discarding the bones and skin. Tear the meat into bite-size pieces. Set aside.

In a 3-quart saucepan, heat the olive oil. Add the onion, celery, and mushrooms and cook until soft. Stir in the flour, pepper, and nutmeg. Continue to cook until the sauce is bubbly. Remove from the heat and gradually stir in the chicken broth and wine. Return to the heat and cook, stirring continuously, until the sauce thickens. Add the chicken, carrots, and peas, and stir. Season with salt to taste. Spread evenly in a 9-inch deep-dish pie pan.

Remove the pastry from the refrigerator and roll out on a floured board into a 12-inch circle. Place the pastry over the chicken mixture, and trim and flute the edge. Cut slits in the top for steam to escape. (At this point, the pie can be refrigerated and baked several hours later or the next day.) In a small bowl, beat together the reserved egg white and 1 teaspoon water. Brush the crust with the egg mixture. Bake for 30 to 40 minutes or until the pastry is golden and the filling is bubbling. Allow to cool for about 10 minutes before cutting.

Chicken Marsala

Serves 4

This dish is best served with rice or pasta.

MERRY "LAMBIE" CALHOUN CARTER

2 tablespoons olive oil

4 boneless, skinless chicken breasts, pounded to ¼ inch thick

1½ cups sliced mushrooms

1 medium onion, chopped

3 cloves garlic, minced

⅓ cup dry marsala wine

4 teaspoons cornstarch

1 teaspoon dried basil

½ teaspoon salt

Dash pepper

⅔ cup chicken broth

Susie Calhoun, Nancy Mueller, Kim Bonde, Merry Carter, Melanie Vieux Celebrating the harvest at Wente Vineyards, 1987

In a large skillet over medium-high heat, heat the oil. Add the chicken and brown it on both sides. Remove the chicken to a plate; add the mushrooms, onion, and garlic to the skillet. Sauté until lightly browned, stirring frequently. Add the wine and bring it to a boil. In a small bowl, mix together the cornstarch, basil, salt, pepper, and broth until smooth. Add the mixture to the skillet and stir, coating all the vegetables with the cornstarch mixture. Bring to a gentle boil and return the chicken breasts to the skillet. Decrease the heat to low, cover, and simmer for 5 minutes or until the chicken is cooked through.

Poached Salmon with Sour Cream Dill Sauce

Serves 2

I would take this dinner up to Granny after Papa died in 1986. We enjoyed eating the salmon with steamed new potatoes and green beans while looking at Cedar Mountain as the sun set.

SUSIE CALHOUN

¾ cup water

¾ cup white wine (Concannon Chardonnay or Sauvignon Blanc)

1½ tablespoons plus ¾ teaspoon freshly squeezed lemon juice

Peel of ½ juiced lemon

1 bay leaf

3 or 4 fresh sprigs parsley

2 (1-inch) salmon fillets (6 ounces each)

¼ cup sour cream

½ teaspoon fresh or 1½ teaspoons dried dill weed

Salt and pepper

¼ teaspoon prepared mustard, preferably Dijon

Little Laina Carter, Granny, Susie Calhoun, and Whitney Ione Carter, 1996

In a large skillet over high heat, combine the water, wine, 1½ tablespoons lemon juice, lemon peel, bay leaf, and parsley and bring to a boil. Add the salmon fillets, making sure they are covered by the poaching liquid. If not, add equal parts water and wine to cover. Lower the heat, cover, and simmer for 8 to 10 minutes or until the fish barely flakes with a fork and the centers are moist. (Add more water if needed.) Meanwhile, in a small bowl, combine the sour cream, dill, the remaining ¾ teaspoon lemon juice, salt, pepper, and mustard. Set aside.

With a slotted spoon, carefully lift the fish onto serving plates. Spoon the sour cream sauce over the fish. 300 calories each!

Sunny Southern California Grilled Fish Tacos

Serves 6

In all my years living at home, I was fed and nourished by my mom and grandmas with healthy, nutritious, tasty foods. But it wasn't until I was in the Navy that I began to taste a lot of really different foods. I found that I loved spicy foods and especially fish. I didn't eat much fish at home, mostly beef and pork if I remember correctly! Living in Hawaii for so many years gave me an appreciation of fish prepared in many different ways. When Jeri and I moved our family to San Diego, I discovered a local favorite, the fish taco. I have tasted many, from countless restaurants and taco stands, and have been making my own at home for quite some time. I often serve them to visitors, and even reluctant recipients say they would gladly come back for more. This recipe is my best "guesstimates." The main thing is to light up the grill, throw on some of your favorite fish and enjoy the day. If you enjoy a beer while grilling, now is the time to do it! The tacos work best with a "make 'em yourself" spread. Put the fillings in serving dishes, and let everyone choose their favorite ingredients. Serve with chips and salsa and maybe some refried beans.

Gary Holm

½ head raw green cabbage, finely shredded
½ pound Cheddar cheese, shredded
½ cup chopped fresh cilantro
2 to 3 limes, cut into wedges
Fresh salsa
Tartar sauce
2 to 3 avocados, cut into slices or small cubes (optional)
2 pounds fish fillets, such as orange roughy, salmon, shark, swordfish, or sea bass
1 to 2 tablespoons olive oil
Pepper
Seasoning mix, such as a "general purpose" or "south of the border" blend (or one of your favorites)
12 to 15 corn tortillas

Prepare a medium-hot fire in a charcoal grill, or preheat a gas grill to medium-high.

Put the cabbage, cheese, cilantro, limes, salsa, tartar sauce, and avocados in individual serving dishes and set them aside until you are ready to eat. Rinse the fish, pat it dry with paper towels, rub it with olive oil, and sprinkle with pepper and spices.

When the grill is ready, place the fish on the rack. Figure about 10 to 15 minutes cooking time per inch of thickness, or 5 to 7 minutes for each side.

Meanwhile, warm up the tortillas by steaming or quickly grilling them on a lightly oiled pancake griddle.

When the fish is done and is cool enough to handle, break it into bite-size pieces and put it in a serving dish. Set all the fillings, fish, and warmed tortillas out for your guests to "build their own" tacos. For example, spread tartar sauce on a warm tortilla, add a layer of shredded cabbage, some fish, and cheese. Top with salsa, cilantro, and plenty of lime juice. Wrap it up, and take a big bite, and enjoy!

Tacos del Mar

Our family is vegetarian, and we entertain a lot. This recipe is a favorite among our meat-eating and vegetarian guests alike. It is not only tasty but healthy, being low in fat and high in protein. I hope you enjoy these tacos as much as we do. We serve them with beans. We like Pico Pica taco sauce, which is found in Mexican markets and in the Mexican section of some grocery stores.

CARLA STEBBINS CANTER

2 pounds fresh firm, flaky white fish fillets
Garlic powder
1 dozen fresh corn tortillas
½ pound Cheddar cheese, shredded
1 head white cabbage, shredded
3 tomatoes, diced
1 medium onion, chopped
Taco sauce

Barbecue, bake, or broil the fish, lightly seasoned with garlic powder to taste. When cool enough to handle, break the fish into bite-size pieces. Warm the corn tortillas over a low flame (do not fry). Build a taco by layering fish, cheese, cabbage, tomatoes, and onions (in that order) on a warm tortilla. Garnish with the taco sauce.

Zippy Fish

Serves 2

In 1988, after many years of planning, and with the goal of finding and fishing the great trout streams of British Columbia, Tilli and Wayne Calhoun, along with their friends Bobbie (Livermore) and Doug Baird, Nancy (Henry) and Jim Lyons, and Joan (Mitchell) Petersen, made the "great Canadian trek." They found beautiful country, friendly people, and excellent uncrowded highways lined with fireweed and other wildflowers. Along with wonderful memories, Tilli brought home this recipe from Prince Rupert, British Columbia.

MERILYN "TILLI" HOLM CALHOUN

Butter for oiling the baking dish
1 pound fish fillets (cod, halibut, or sole)
¼ cup mayonnaise
2 teaspoons hot prepared mustard
2 tablespoons finely chopped onion
Paprika

Preheat the oven to 450°F, and butter a baking dish. Arrange the fillets in a single layer in the baking dish. In a small bowl, combine the mayonnaise, mustard, and onions and spread it evenly over the fillets. Sprinkle with paprika and bake for 10 minutes or until the fish is cooked to your liking.

Margarita Shrimp

Serves 6

This dish can be prepared up to six hours ahead of time.

BECKY CALHOUN FOSTER

5 tablespoons olive oil

1 pound uncooked medium-size
    shrimp, peeled, deveined and
    halved lengthwise

½ cup minced green onions

2 large cloves garlic, minced

¼ cup tequila, plus a little more

¼ cup chopped fresh cilantro

2 tablespoons freshly squeezed lime juice

½ teaspoon margarita salt or coarse salt

Lime wedges, for garnish

Heat the oil in a large, heavy skillet over medium-high heat. Add the shrimp, green onions, and garlic, and sauté until the shrimp turns pink, about 1 minute. Remove from the heat and add the tequila. Return to the heat and bring to a boil, scraping up any browned bits from the bottom of the pan. Transfer to a medium-size bowl, cover tightly, and chill in the refrigerator.

When ready to serve, toss the shrimp with the cilantro, lime juice, and salt. Garnish with the lime wedges.

Crab and Dressing for a Crowd   *Serves 15 to 20 as an appetizer*

Uncle Richie would bring ice chests full of fresh crab to Christmas Eve gatherings and would be busy cracking them from lunch until dinner. This is the dressing he served with the crab. The recipe makes about 3 cups of dressing.

RICH HOLM

Dressing

2 cups mayonnaise

1 cup ketchup

2 teaspoons Worcestershire

10 to 12 large, cleaned, cooked, and
    cracked Dungeness crab

In a mixing bowl, combine the mayonnaise, ketchup, and Worcestershire sauce, and blend well.

Serve the dressing in small bowls along with the crab.

Uncle Richie Holm with cracked crab, Christmas Eve

Crab Cioppino

Serves 4 to 6

This dish is a tradition at Bob and Deanna Holm's Christmas Eve dinner. It was started years ago by Deanna's mother, Laverne Dickey. For bigger gatherings, we usually double the recipe and add shrimp and clams. Upon request, you may be able to purchase the crabs already cleaned, cooked, and cracked. If you do prepare the cioppino with clams and shrimp, add the clams along with the crab and simmer until the clams open. Then add the shrimp and simmer until pink, which will take just a few minutes.

DEANNA DICKEY HOLM

⅓ cup olive oil

1½ stalks celery, diced

1 large onion, diced

1 bunch green onions, white parts only, chopped

2 cloves garlic

1 carrot, grated

1 (1-pound) can tomato purée

2 (8-ounce) cans tomato sauce

2½ cups water

⅓ cup chopped fresh parsley

1 bay leaf

¼ teaspoon dried rosemary

¼ teaspoon dried thyme

4 crabs, cleaned, cooked, and cracked

Heat the oil in a large pot over medium heat. Add the celery and onion and sauté for 10 minutes. Add the garlic, carrot, tomato purée and sauce, water, parsley, bay leaf, rosemary, and thyme and simmer for about an hour. Add the crab and simmer until it is heated through, approximately 15 minutes.

Bobby and Tommy Holm on the diving board at the Circle H Ranch. The high dive was torn down the next day.

Frikadeller (Danish Meatballs)

Makes about 30 meatballs and ¾ cup gravy

This was one of Papa's favorites at Dania Hall events. The Holm family enjoyed going to the Frikadeller Dinner, hosted by the Dania Lodge. The meatballs were oblong and a bit flattened. They were served with gravy, creamed potatoes, and red cabbage.

Frikadellar is a Danish dish with many variations. Traditionally, the meatballs are made with ground veal, pork, and beef. My recipe does not use veal, but you could replace some of the ground meat with veal. The mixture is formed into balls and then pan-fried with oil or butter. I use olive oil. The gravy recipe makes three-quarters of a cup of gravy—you may want to double the recipe if you'd like more gravy.

Some cooks use tomato juice instead of the milk or cream. And, you can use egg whites instead of whole eggs.

SUSIE CALHOUN

Meatballs
1½ pounds ground beef
½ pound ground pork
1 cup finely chopped red onion
½ cup bread crumbs
1 teaspoon salt
½ teaspoon pepper
½ teaspoon grated nutmeg
2 tablespoons flour
2 eggs
1 tablespoon cream or milk
2 tablespoons olive oil or butter

Gravy
3 tablespoons flour
1 tablespoon pan drippings from
    the meatballs
¾ cup cream or milk
Salt and pepper

In a large bowl, combine the beef and pork. Add the chopped onion and mix well with your hands. Add the bread crumbs, salt, pepper, nutmeg, flour, eggs, and cream. Mix well. Shape into oblong egg-sized meatballs.

Heat the oil in a large skillet over medium heat. When the oil is hot, add the meatballs. Brown the outsides, then continue cooking until they are cooked through, 8 to 10 minutes. Remove the meatballs from the skillet, drain on paper towels, and keep warm.

In the same skillet, brown the flour in the drippings. Slowly add the cream, stirring continuously, until the mixture thickens and becomes the consistency of gravy. Season with salt and pepper to taste.

After selling Fair View and moving to Mines Road, Dick and Ione were able to travel with Farm Bureau Tours around the world, going to Scandinavia, Australia, New Zealand, Fiji, Hawaii, and Alaska. They traveled with Creight and Margaret Baxter and the McCumbers. Their suitcases were always brimming with dolls and mementos upon their return, and the grandkids would all yell, "What did you bring us?"

Beef Brisket

Kathie George from a recipe given to her by a friend

¼ cup flour

1 teaspoon salt

½ teaspoon pepper

1 teaspoon paprika

4 pounds beef brisket

2 tablespoons oil

1 large yellow onion, chopped

1 (8-ounce) can tomato sauce

½ cup beef broth or red wine

12 small boiling onions, peeled

2 tablespoons sugar

4 to 8 carrots, cut into chunks

In a pie plate or large, flat dish, combine the flour, salt, pepper, and paprika. Lightly dust the beef with this mixture. Heat the oil in a large skillet over medium-high heat and brown the meat and onion. Add the tomato sauce and broth or wine. Cover, decrease the heat to low, and simmer for 2 to 3 hours. After 2 hours, add the onions. Add the sugar and carrots for the last 30 minutes of cooking.

As an alternative to this stovetop method, this dish can also be roasted in a 325° oven for 2 to 3 hours.

Skewered Steak Strips Sauterne

Serves 4 to 5

This is Don's favorite recipe for grilling. We usually double or triple the recipe depending on how many of the boys will be at home!

Del Shult Neely

¾ cup sauterne

1 tablespoon soy sauce

1½ pounds flank steak, less than 1 inch thick

1 clove garlic, minced

2 tablespoons steak sauce

2 tablespoons butter

1 tablespoon brown sugar

2 teaspoons dry mustard

8 to 10 whole mushrooms

Skewers

In a small bowl, combine the sauterne and soy sauce to make a marinade. Cut the steak against the grain into long 1-inch wide strips. In a nonmetallic bowl or plastic bag, pour the marinade over the meat and marinate at least 2 hours at room temperature or overnight in the refrigerator.

When ready to grill, prepare a medium-hot fire in a charcoal grill, or preheat a gas grill to medium-high. Drain the marinade from the beef, reserving the marinade. In a saucepan over medium-high heat, combine the reserved marinade with the garlic, steak sauce, butter, brown sugar, and mustard to make a basting sauce. Heat to just boiling and remove from the heat. Thread the beef strips onto skewers, alternating the beef with the mushrooms. Grill for 15 to 20 minutes, basting frequently.

Beef Short Ribs

Serves 4

This recipe comes from Liz Thome Jenson, a dear friend of the Ken Calhoun family. It is great on those rainy football game days. If you like, you can add cut-up potatoes and carrots for a whole meal. There are two temperatures and cooking times noted—I prefer the "low and slow" method, as the finished ribs are more tender.

CINDY CALHOUN MILLER

3 to 5 pounds short ribs, trimmed of fat

Sauce
¼ cup apple cider vinegar
1 cup tomato ketchup
3 tablespoons Worcestershire sauce
1 teaspoon mustard
2 tablespoons sugar
½ cup water
2 teaspoons salt
1 yellow onion, chopped

Preheat the oven to 325°F or 250°F, depending on your preferred cooking time.

In a large frying pan, brown the short ribs and pour off the fat. You may have to do this in batches.

In a bowl, combine the vinegar, ketchup, Worcestershire sauce, mustard, sugar, water, salt, and onion.

Put the ribs in a large, heavy, lidded sauce pan. Coat the ribs with the sauce and cover the pan with the lid. Bake for 1 hour at 325°F or 4 hours at 250°F.

Jeff Calhoun, Cindy Calhoun Miller, Vivian and Ken Calhoun, Becky Calhoun, and Kenny Calhoun at the wedding of Cindy Calhoun and Troy Miller.

171

Swedish Meatballs

Makes 6 servings

BETTY SORENSON PALMER

3 tablespoons butter or margarine
1 large onion, chopped
½ cup milk
3 slices fresh bread, with crust
1½ pounds lean ground beef
2 eggs
1 teaspoon salt
½ teaspoon freshly ground black pepper
Butter or oil for frying
1 tablespoon flour
1½ cups beef bouillon
½ cup half and half
2 tablespoons sherry (optional)

In a large skillet over medium heat, melt the butter, add the onions and sauté until golden brown. Pour the milk into a pie plate and add the bread. Soak until the bread absorbs the milk. In a mixing bowl, combine the beef with the onions, bread, eggs, salt, and pepper. Blend well. Form the mixture into 1-inch balls.

In the same skillet over medium heat, add the butter or oil, if needed, and fry the meatballs until evenly browned. Shake the skillet often to keep the balls round. Remove the meatballs from the skillet and place on a warm platter.

Add the flour to the remaining juices in the skillet and blend. Stir in the bouillon and cream. Cook, stirring constantly, until the sauce is well blended and has thickened. Add the sherry and correct the seasoning if necessary. Add the meatballs, cover the pan, and simmer for 15 minutes or until the meatballs are warmed through.

Back: Jim Fallon, Russ Rasmussen, Rich Palmer, Tony George, Dick Holm, Fred Shepherd, Les Holm Sr.
Kneeling: Jim Holm, Louie Dentici
Seated: Clarence Groth, Hank Neely
Standing: Otto Fachner

Stegt Julegaas (Roast Goose for Christmas) *Serves 6 to 8*

This is a popular Danish holiday dish. It is served with red cabbage and browned potatoes. Select a young goose as older ones tend to be tough.

About 1 pound dried, pitted prunes
1 (10-pound to 12-pound) goose, singed
Salt
2 pounds tart apples, peeled, cored and quartered
½ cup flour, or more as needed
6 tablespoons butter

From front, clockwise: Danish cousins Mark, Simon, Rune, Tom, and Charlotte Koch Hvilsted, with Ione at Christmas dinner, 1983

In a small bowl, cover the prunes with boiling water and let soak for about 20 minutes or until plumped. Drain and cut in half.

Preheat the oven to 450°F. Carefully wash the goose inside and out with hot water, and salt it both inside and out. In a bowl, combine the apples and prunes. Loosely stuff the goose with the fruit mixture and close the opening with small skewers or kitchen string. Place the goose in a roasting pan and roast for 45 minutes. Remove from the oven and drain all the fat from the pan. Sprinkle the goose all over with flour. Return to the oven and lower the temperature to 350°F.

In a small pot over high heat, combine 1 cup water and the butter. Heat until the butter is melted completely, then whisk together. When the flour on the goose has browned, start basting it with the water-butter mixture. Baste frequently. Sprinkle lightly with flour after each basting as that absorbs any excess grease. Allow a total roasting time of 20 minutes per pound, including the 45 minutes at high heat. Juices should run clear when the thigh is pierced with a sharp knife.

Carl Holm's sister Charlotte and Stanley Koch, Axel, and Otto in Denmark

173

Seasoned Barbecued Duck

Serves 6 to 8

This is a favorite main course that my husband Troy likes to prepare when we entertain during the winter months. Since Troy enjoys duck hunting, he is usually absent from many Sunday morning church services, but he is forgiven as our friends look forward to invitations to our duck dinners. Many of our friends' children especially enjoy the duck just as much as their parents do.

CINDY CALHOUN MILLER

4 (3- to 4-pound) whole,
    cleaned ducks
Peanut oil
Garlic salt
Lemon pepper
8 to 10 garlic cloves, minced

Prepare a hot, indirect fire in a charcoal grill by building the fire in the center, and then moving the briquettes to the edges. This leaves the center of the rack with no briquettes under it, which prevents the coals from flaming up as the duck fat renders. Wash the ducks, pat dry (so the oil and seasonings will adhere), and prick the skin of each duck all over with a fork so the fat can render. Rub them with peanut oil, inside and out. Season heavily inside and out with garlic salt, lemon pepper, and minced garlic.

When the fire is ready (the coals should be red hot) place the ducks in the center of the rack, breast up. Cover and barbecue for about 30 minutes without touching or turning. Add briquettes, if necessary, to the coals on the edges. Be sure to avoid direct heat under the birds. Continue to cook until the meat reaches a minimum of 165°F on a meat thermometer, about another 30 minutes (depending on your grill). The meat will be pink below the skin. Remove from the grill. Cut each duck in half (neck to tail) with poultry shears. Cut away the skin and serve the meat only.

Troy, Cindy, Callie, and Max Miller

Wild Pheasant

Here is a recipe for preparing wild pheasant. I think three pheasant serve eight people nicely. I have used five pheasant, doubled the recipe, and served sixteen. The recipe also works well with chicken. Be sure to use the broth left in the bottom of the roasting pan to make gravy. A little rice alongside is great, too.

KEN AND VIVIAN CALHOUN

3 pheasant, cleaned and cut into pieces
Olive oil for frying
Flour for dredging
2 cups chopped green onion
2 cups chopped celery
2 cups chopped fresh parsley
1 cup low-salt chicken stock
1½ cups sauterne or sherry (or any dry, white wine)
½ teaspoon salt
¼ teaspoon pepper
½ teaspoon paprika

Preheat the oven to 350°F.

Flour the pheasant pieces. In a frying pan over medium heat, brown the pieces on both sides.

Meanwhile, in a bowl, combine the green onions, celery, and parsley. When the pheasant pieces are browned, transfer them to a 2- to 3-quart ovenproof casserole with a lid, and evenly cover them with the vegetable mixture.

In a small bowl, combine the chicken stock, sauterne, salt, pepper, and paprika. Pour the mixture over the pheasant.

Cover and bake for 2 hours. Check occasionally to make sure the broth does not boil away. If it does, add a little water or wine, or both. Bake until meat is tender and cooked through.

The Calhoun cousins, circa 1968
Becky, Kenny, Susie, Grandpa Reg,
Nancy, Cindy, Merry, and Jeff Calhoun

Ken and Wayne Calhoun

Grandpa's Quail

Hunting has always been part of our family. I can remember one outing with my grandfather, Reg Calhoun, when we drove up to a cabin on Pine Ridge above Lake Del Valle in Livermore. The two of us were in his Scout; he was driving at a decent clip and the road was steep and very bumpy. At that time, I was so light that I hit my head on the roof of the Scout! I found this recipe in my grandfather's elegant handwriting. I believe it was given to him by his son Ken.

NANCY CALHOUN MUELLER

Nancy with both grandpas—
Dick Holm and Reg Calhoun,
1984

6 whole quail
2 tablespoons olive oil, plus more as needed
Salt and pepper
4 cloves garlic, minced
1 medium yellow onion, chopped
½ pound fresh mushrooms, sliced
¼ cup fresh sage, coarsely chopped
¼ cup fresh rosemary, chopped
½ cup fresh parsley, coarsely chopped
½ cup white wine

In a large pan over medium-high heat, brown the quail in olive oil, adding salt and pepper to taste. While they are cooking, sprinkle them with the garlic. Once they are browned, sprinkle the vegetables and herbs over the quail. Add the wine, cover and simmer at a very low heat for 1 hour, or until the quail are tender.

Venison Jerky

Making jerky is a great way to use the very flavorful and less expensive cuts of meat. Traditionally, jerky is air-dried, but I make it in my oven, and it comes out great. Some ovens don't go as low as the 120°F called for in the recipe. In that case, turn your oven down as low as it will go. You may have to reduce the total oven time. Keep an eye on the meat toward the end of the cooking time and remove it from the oven when it is shriveled and black. Feel free to be creative with your herb and spice mixture. The meat is easier to cut into strips if you partially freeze it first.

SUSIE CALHOUN

4 pounds fresh boneless meat, trimmed of fat

⅓ to ½ cup herb and spice mixture (I use salt, pepper, thyme, oregano, marjoram, and basil)

Preheat the oven to 120°F. Cut the meat along the grain into strips about ½ inch thick and 1 inch wide. Spread the strips out on your work surface, sprinkle the herb mixture on 1 side and pound with a meat hammer. Turn the strips over and repeat. Spread the strips on a cookie sheet or similar flat pan (some people just spread them directly on the wire racks in their ovens) and place in the oven, leaving the door slightly ajar so the moisture can escape. After about 4 hours, turn the meat over. Bake for an additional 3 to 4 hours. When the meat is shriveled and black, it's done. Remove the jerky from the oven when it is still bendable; it will get more brittle as it cools.

Easy Pork Chops with Gravy

Serves 4

These chops are perfect served over rice or egg noodles.

STACI HOLM BROWN

¼ cup flour for dredging
Garlic salt
Pepper
2 tablespoons olive oil
4 (1-inch) thick pork chops
1 (10.5-ounce) can cream of mushroom soup
1 (8-ounce) can chicken broth
1 (1-ounce) packet onion soup mix

In a dish or pie pan, combine the flour with garlic salt and pepper to taste. Heat the olive oil in a skillet over medium heat. Coat each pork chop with the seasoned flour. Brown the pork chops, about 2 minutes each side. Remove the chops from the skillet and set aside. Combine the mushroom soup, broth, and soup mix in the skillet, and stir well. Return the pork chops to the skillet, cover, and simmer 7 to 10 minutes on each side or until the chops are cooked through. The total cooking time will depend on the size and thickness of your chops.

Cactus Stew

You can find jars of cactus (nopales) in the Mexican food section of the grocery store. This stew is best served over Spanish- or Mexican-style rice. Warm tortillas are great, too!

MARIO GARCIA

2 tablespoons butter, or cooking-oil spray

4 cloves garlic, plus more if desired

3 to 6 pounds beef chuck, cut into
    bite-size cubes

1 to 1½ onions, diced

1½ teaspoons salt

Finely chopped jalapeños

4 (8-ounce) cans tomato sauce

2 (14.5-ounce) cans stewed tomatoes

1½ teaspoons paprika

1 tablespoon ground cumin

1½ teaspoons chili powder

5 to 10 russet potatoes, cut into
    bite-size cubes

2 (30-ounce) jars chopped nopales
    (cactus), drained and rinsed

Heat a large pot over medium heat. Melt the butter in the pot (or spray with Pam).

Using a garlic press, press the garlic into the pot. Add more garlic if you like. Quickly add the beef and onions. Season with salt and jalapeños to taste. Cook until the beef is nice and brown, stirring frequently. Add the tomato sauce and stewed tomatoes. Season with paprika, cumin, and chili powder and stir well. Add the potatoes. Bring to a light boil, cover, reduce the heat, and simmer for 30 to 35 minutes. Stir occasionally. Stir in the cactus and simmer for another 30 to 35 minutes. Stir every 10 minutes. Check the seasoning and add salt if needed. Let the stew cook on low heat for another 20 minutes; continue to stir occasionally, then serve.

Cookies, Cakes, Candies, and More

Granny and Papa
Fiftieth Wedding Anniversary

Lemon Meringue Pie

Makes one 9-inch pie

This pie is a very special treat for our family, neighbors, and friends. The recipe is based on one from an old cookbook of my mother, Gertrude Foxworthy. The book was called Fifty-Two Sunday Dinners *by Elizabeth O. Hiller, dated 1913. As it was passed from generation to generation, we have all made some changes; we think our present version is great.*

MARY FOXWORTHY RASMUSSEN

1½ cups sugar
¼ cup cornstarch
¼ teaspoon salt
1½ teaspoons grated lemon zest
2 cups hot water
3 large eggs, separated
⅓ cup freshly squeezed lemon juice
2 tablespoons butter, cut into small pieces
1 prebaked 9-inch pastry shell
¼ cup powdered sugar
½ teaspoon cream of tartar

In a heavy saucepan, combine the sugar, cornstarch, salt, and lemon rind; add the hot water gradually, blending well. Cook over low heat, stirring constantly, until the mixture is smooth and thick enough to coat the back of a spoon. Remove from the heat. In a bowl, whisk together the egg yolks and lemon juice. Whisk about 2 tablespoons of the hot mixture into the egg yolks. Still off the heat, whisk this egg yolk mixture back into the thickened mixture in the saucepan, whisking constantly. Add the butter and stir until it has melted. Cool, stirring occasionally. When it has cooled, pour it into the pastry shell.

Preheat the oven to 350°F.

To make the meringue, beat the egg whites until stiff in a mixing bowl. Whisk in the powdered sugar and cream of tartar. Top the pie with the meringue and bake for 12 to 15 minutes, or until the peaks are lightly browned.

Granny's Apple Pie

Granny's apple pies were the best! I wanted to learn to make them just like she did, so one day we made one together. I had her measure out all the ingredients, even the ones she measured with her hands. I think the secret of her pies was to use thinly sliced apple and a thin crust. Granny suggested using pippin apples, which are now hard to find. Granny Smiths are a good substitute. I only make these pies for Thanksgiving. They taste really good—but not as good as Granny's!

Wendy Neely Howe

Pastry crust
2 cups sifted all-purpose flour
1 teaspoon salt
⅔ cup shortening
5 to 7 tablespoons cold water

Filling
¾ cup sugar
1 teaspoon cinnamon
¼ teaspoon grated nutmeg
5 to 6 tart apples, peeled, cored, and thinly sliced (Granny Smiths or pippins)
3 tablespoons butter, cut into small pieces

Preheat the oven to 450°F.

To make the crust: Sift the flour and salt together into a bowl. Using a pastry blender, cut in the shortening until the pieces are the size of small peas. Sprinkle in the water, 1 tablespoon at a time, gently mixing with a fork. Continue until all the flour is moistened and the dough almost pulls away from the sides of the bowl. Divide the dough in half and shape into 2 flattened rounds on a lightly floured surface. With a flour-covered rolling pin, roll the dough into a disk 2 inches larger than the pie pan. The dough is best when rolled to approximately ⅛ inch thick. Fold the pastry disk into quarters; place it in the pie pan and unfold. Trim the overhanging edge of the pastry ½ inch from the rim of the pan. Roll out the second round of dough, dust it lightly with flour, fold it into quarters and set aside.

To make the filling: In a small bowl, mix together the sugar, cinnamon, and nutmeg. Fill the pastry-lined pie pan with half of the apples and sprinkle half of the sugar mixture over the apples. Add the remaining apples and sprinkle the rest of the sugar mixture over them. The apples should be an inch above the pan rim. Dot the top of the pie with the butter pieces. Place the second crust over the filling and unfold. Trim the overhanging edge of the pastry 1 inch from the rim of the pan. Seal the top and bottom crusts together by pressing a fork around the edge. Cut slits into the top crust so the steam can escape. Cover the edge with a strip of aluminum foil to prevent excessive browning; remove the foil the last 15 minutes of baking. Bake 10 to 15 minutes at 450°F. Turn the oven down to 350°F and bake 30 to 45 minutes longer or until the crust is golden brown and the filling is bubbling. Let cool before serving.

Applesauce Cake

Makes one 5- by 10-inch cake

This is an old recipe which has been passed along through the Carter family.

VELMA CARTER, *mother-in-law of Merry Calhoun Carter*

⅓ cup shortening, at room temperature plus more for oiling the pan

1⅔ cups sifted all-purpose flour

1⅓ cups sugar

¼ teaspoon baking powder

1 teaspoon baking soda

¾ teaspoon salt

¼ teaspoon ground cloves

½ teaspoon ground cinnamon

¼ teaspoon ground allspice

⅓ cup water

⅓ cup chopped nuts

⅔ cup raisins or chopped dates

1 cup thick, unsweetened applesauce

1 large egg

The Carter family in
St. Joseph, Missouri
Back: Dennis, Darrell, Susan,
and Brent
Front: Velma, Whitney, and Laina

Preheat the oven to 350°F and butter a 5- by 10-inch baking pan.

Sift together the flour, sugar, baking powder, soda, salt, cloves, cinnamon, and allspice into the large bowl of a mixer. Add the shortening, water, nuts, raisins, and applesauce, and beat on slow to medium speed for 2 minutes. Scrape down the sides and bottom of the bowl frequently. Add the egg and continue to beat for 2 more minutes, scraping down the sides of the bowl. Pour the batter into the pan and bake for 50 to 55 minutes, or until a toothpick inserted in the center comes out clean. Let cool before serving.

Boiled Raisin Spice Cake

Makes one 9- by 13-inch cake

Choose you favorite cream cheese frosting and frost the cake when it is cool.

BLANCHE RASMUSSEN GEORGE

1 cup salad oil plus more for oiling the pan

3½ cups flour plus more for dusting the pan

2 cups seedless raisins

2 cups water

2 cups sugar

2 eggs, slightly beaten

½ teaspoon salt

2 teaspoons baking soda

2 teaspoons ground cinnamon

2 teaspoons ground allspice

1 teaspoon ground cloves

½ to 1 cup chopped nuts (optional)

Preheat the oven to 375°F, and oil and flour a 9- by 13- by 2-inch baking pan.

In a pot over high heat, combine the raisins and the water. Bring the mixture to a boil, remove from the heat, and stir the cup of oil. Cool the mixture to lukewarm. Whisk in the sugar and eggs. Sift together the flour, salt, baking soda, cinnamon, allspice, and cloves. Add to the liquid and stir until smooth. Add the nuts, if desired. Pour the batter into the baking pan and bake for 50 minutes, or until an inserted cake tester or toothpick comes out clean. Cool the cake before frosting.

Tony and Blanche George at the Circle H Ranch

Tony and Blanche George were the caretakers at the Circle H Ranch for many years. They lived in a very small cabin on the ranch, which seemed like a museum to us. On the walls were mounted bobcats and other stuffed animals. They had a menagerie of animals, including the parakeets and canaries Blanche raised in aviaries in the yard. Tony often demonstrated extreme patience with us on cattle drives when he had to break up fights, saddle our horses when our saddles fell off, open gates for us, chase the cows we let get away, and so on. We learned our first curse words from Tony. "You damn buggers!" he'd yell at the cattle. We got our mouths washed out with soap when we repeated those words at home.
— Merry Carter

Texas Sheet Cake

This recipe is great to take to a barbecue or picnic, and it always disappears quickly.

GAYLE FACHNER DILTZ

Cake

1 cup (2 sticks) butter or margarine plus butter for oiling the pan

1 cup water

¼ cup unsweetened cocoa powder

2 cups all-purpose flour

2 cups sugar

½ teaspoon salt

1 teaspoon baking soda

2 eggs

½ cup sour cream

Frosting

½ cup (1 stick) butter or margarine

¼ cup unsweetened cocoa powder

6 tablespoons milk

2¾ cups powdered sugar

1 teaspoon vanilla extract

1 cup chopped nuts

Preheat the oven to 375°F and butter a large, 12- by 16-inch baking sheet with a lip.

To make the cake, combine the butter, water, and cocoa in a pot over high heat and bring it to a boil. Remove from the heat. In another bowl, combine the flour, sugar, salt, and baking soda. Using a mixer, add the flour mixture to the cocoa mixture and beat until smooth. Beat in the eggs and sour cream and mix until well blended. Pour the batter into the baking sheet and bake for 20 minutes or until an inserted toothpick comes out clean.

To make the frosting, combine the butter, cocoa, and milk in a pot over high heat and bring it to a boil. Remove from the heat and stir in the powdered sugar, vanilla, and nuts. Mix until smooth. Pour the frosting over the cake as soon as it comes out of the oven and spread it evenly with a spatula. Let it cool before serving.

The Diltz brothers: Tony and twins Donnie and Ronnie. All were stationed on the U.S.S. Picket, 1962.

Broken Glass Torte

Makes one 9-inch torte

I got this recipe at my first real job. I was working for the Division of Highways—now Caltrans—in San Francisco in 1964, and I have been making it ever since. Our oldest daughter, Kristine, requests this for her birthday every year. She was born on December 19 and is adamant about not having anything related to Christmas included in her birthday celebration, including her cake or gift wrappings. So, every year I have to wrack my brain to come up with a unique decoration for the top of her cake. The cake is quite plain looking if you don't do a little creative decorating. I think fresh flowers are the prettiest, but you can use candy or sprinkles, too. Use any three flavors of Jell-o you prefer—I usually use orange, red, and green so I get a variety of color. When the cake is sliced, it resembles stained glass.

GAYLE FACHNER DILTZ

3 (2.75-ounce) packages Jell-o
   (3 different flavors)
1 cup pineapple juice
1 envelope unflavored gelatin
2 pints whipping cream (4 cups)
¼ cup sugar
1 teaspoon vanilla extract
1 angel food cake, torn or cut
   into chunks

Keeping the flavors separate, prepare the 3 packages of Jell-o, using only 1½ cups water per package. Pour each flavor into a small, shallow pan. Ice cube trays from the refrigerator are a good size. Put the pans of Jell-o in the refrigerator to set up.

In a small pot, bring the pineapple juice to a boil. In a medium bowl, dissolve the gelatin in ¼ cup cold water. Add the juice to the gelatin, stir well, and cool.

Remove the Jell-o from the refrigerator and cut each flavor up into ½-inch cubes. In another bowl, whip 1 pint of the whipping cream to soft peaks. Add the sugar and vanilla, and fold into the juice mixture. Gently fold the Jell-o cubes into the cream mixture.

Line the bottom and sides of a 9-inch springform pan with the pieces of angel food cake. Pour the cream and Jell-o mixture into the lined pan, and let it chill in the refrigerator for 6 to 12 hours. Turn out onto a serving plate. Whip the remaining pint of whipping cream, frost the torte, and then decorate it.

The next generation of ranch hands
Kevin Avila, son of Korry Diltz with
Caitlyn Fachner, daughter of Dan and
Christine Fachner, 1995

Buttermilk Bundt Cake

This recipe was a favorite of the Navy wives who lived on Midway Island in the North Pacific Ocean. The ingredients are simple and were usually available in the commissary, which was open only five days a week during daytime hours. The next closest store was 1,150 miles away in Honolulu, and the plane flew in only twice a week. So you can see, a Navy wife did a lot of planning ahead, if only to bake a cake! I made this large cake many times for Granny's Christmas luncheons, mostly because the leftovers freeze well. Also, Wayne Calhoun bolstered my ego each time I brought it by telling me how much he liked it.

RAE SVEEN

1 cup shortening, plus more for
    oiling the pan
3 cups sugar
6 eggs, well-beaten
1 teaspoon almond extract
½ teaspoon vanilla extract
3 cups all-purpose flour
¼ teaspoon salt
1 cup buttermilk combined with
    ¼ teaspoon baking soda

Preheat the oven to 350°F and oil a 10-inch Bundt pan.

In a bowl, cream together the shortening and sugar. Add the eggs, almond and vanilla extracts, and mix well.

In another bowl, combine the flour and salt. Stir the flour into the egg mixture, a little at a time, alternating with the buttermilk, until all the ingredients are well combined. Pour the batter into the Bundt pan and bake for approximately 1½ hours, or until a toothpick inserted in the middle comes out clean. Let cool before serving.

Éclair Cake

I brought this "cake" for the Fourth of July picnic one year and folks said it really tasted like éclairs! A co-worker passed the recipe on to me. I've "lightened" it a little, but not too much!

JANET FACHNER VON TOUSSAINT

Cake
Butter for oiling the pan
1 (1-pound) box reduced-fat graham crackers (you will have some left over)
2 (3.4-ounce) packages instant French vanilla or instant vanilla pudding
3½ cups milk (skim, low-fat, or regular)
1 (8-ounce) container Lite Cool Whip, thawed

Frosting
2 ounces unsweetened chocolate
2 teaspoons light corn syrup
2 teaspoons vanilla extract
3 tablespoons butter or margarine, softened
1½ cups powdered sugar
3 tablespoons milk

Butter a 9- by 13-inch baking dish. Line the bottom of the pan with whole graham crackers. (They don't have to fit exactly or be beautiful.)

In a mixing bowl, combine the pudding and milk. Using a mixer, beat at medium speed for 2 minutes. Fold in the Cool Whip.

Pour half the mixture over the graham crackers, then place a second layer of crackers over the pudding. Pour the remaining pudding mixture over this layer and cover with more crackers. Chill for 2 hours.

Meanwhile, make the frosting. Melt the chocolate in the microwave oven. Or, chop the chocolate and melt over hot water in a double boiler. Combine the chocolate, corn syrup, vanilla, butter, sugar, and milk in a mixing bowl. Beat until smooth. Frost the chilled cake and refrigerate for 24 hours. Keep refrigerated until your are ready to serve. To serve, cut into squares.

Back: Mabel Holm Jorgensen with Lynn Jorgensen on lap, Carl Jorgensen, Danny Fachner
Front: Randy Regnolds, Carol Jorgensen holding Billy Jorgensen, Gayle Fachner holding Janet Fachner, Vickie Regnolds

Uncles' Special Cake

Makes one 9- by 13-inch cake

As a girl, my mother, Phyllis Jorgensen Fachner, made this cake when she helped out at Aunt Ione and Uncle Dick's ranch. She named it "Uncles' Special" because Uncle Les and Uncle Dick liked it so much. Mother says there was rarely any left over. She made it from scratch because "they didn't have cake mixes back then," and provided me with this modern version.

JANET FACHNER VON TOUSSAINT

1 box yellow cake mix
4 to 5 tablespoons butter or margarine
¼ cup evaporated milk
¾ cup packed brown sugar
¾ cup chopped walnuts or
   toasted almonds
¾ cup shredded coconut

Preheat the oven to 350°F.

Bake the cake in a 9- by 13-inch cake pan according to the package instructions.

While the cake is baking, melt the butter in a saucepan over medium heat. Add the milk and brown sugar and cook until the sugar is dissolved. Stir in the nuts and coconut. Carefully spread the mixture on top of the baked cake. Bake for about 10 minutes or until the topping is caramelized and lightly browned.

Microwave Chocolate Peanut Clusters

Makes 60 pieces

I make these every year to include in holiday goodie baskets. They are quick and easy and can be refrigerated until you need them for gift-giving.

JANET FACHNER VON TOUSSAINT

1 (10- to 12-ounce) package semisweet
   chocolate chips
1 (16-ounce package) vanilla Candy Quick
   candy coating (in the baking section)
1 (16-ounce) jar unsalted, dry-roasted
   peanuts

Put the chocolate chips and the Candy Quick in a large, microwave-proof bowl or casserole and cover. Microwave on high for 4 minutes. Stir. Microwave for additional time, if needed, until completely melted. Stir in the nuts and mix well.

Drop the batter by teaspoonfuls onto waxed paper, being careful not to make the clusters too big. Let them harden. Store in a covered container.

Walnut Bars

This is one of mom's favorites. It makes a huge batch. They are sinfully delicious and great for the holidays. No calories of course!

BECKY CALHOUN FOSTER

Crust
2 cups plus 2 tablespoons
    all-purpose flour

1 cup butter or margarine, softened

½ cup cornstarch

½ cup sugar

Filling
1 pound box brown sugar (2¼ cups
    packed)

4 eggs, slightly beaten

1 (14-ounce) bag sweetened shredded
    coconut, or less (about 6 cups)

½ teaspoon baking powder

4 cups chopped walnuts

Frosting
8 ounces cream cheese, softened

2 teaspoons vanilla extract

½ cup (1 stick) butter or margarine, at
    room temperature

1 pound box powdered sugar (3½ to
    4 cups)

Preheat the oven to 300°F.

To make the crust: In a bowl, combine 2 cups flour, butter, cornstarch, and sugar. Mix until crumbly. Evenly pack this mixture into a 15- by 12-inch jelly roll pan, forming a crust, and bake for 15 minutes.

Meanwhile, in a bowl, combine the remaining 2 tablespoons flour, brown sugar, eggs, coconut, and baking powder. Mix well. Add the walnuts to the mixture. When the crust is ready, remove it from the oven and carefully spread the walnut mixture over the hot crust. Bake 15 to 20 minutes more. Cool.

To make the frosting: In a bowl, combine the cream cheese, vanilla, butter, and powdered sugar. Spread the frosting over the cooled walnut mixture and cut into 2-inch square bars.

Becky Foster and daughter Kelsie at the Circle H Ranch

 *Brownies*

IONE TEETER HOLM

⅓ cup butter, plus more to oil the pan
1 cup sugar
2 squares semisweet chocolate, melted
1 teaspoon vanilla extract
2 eggs, well beaten
¾ cup all-purpose flour
½ teaspoon baking powder
½ cup walnuts, chopped

Makes about 15 brownies

Preheat the oven to 350°F. Butter and flour a 7- by 11-inch pan.

In a bowl, cream together the butter and sugar. Add the chocolate, vanilla, and eggs. Fold in the flour, baking powder, and walnuts. Pour the batter into the pan and bake for 35 minutes, or until the brownies are dry on top and almost firm to the touch. Cool and cut into squares.

Cream Cheese Brownies

SANDY SPORTS HOLM

Butter for oiling the pan
Flour for dusting the pan
1 package German chocolate cake mix
1 (8-ounce) package cream cheese, softened
1 egg
½ cup sugar
½ cup milk chocolate chips, plus ¼ cup to sprinkle on top
¼ chopped nuts (optional)

Makes about 24 brownies

Preheat the oven to 350°F. Butter and flour a 15½- by 10½- by 1-inch jelly roll pan.

Prepare the cake mix as directed on the package, and pour the batter into the pan. In a small bowl, mix together the cream cheese, egg, sugar, and chocolate chips. Using a tablespoon, drop spoonfuls of the mixture onto the batter. Cut through the batter with a knife or metal spatula several times to create a marbled effect. Sprinkle with additional chocolate chips and chopped nuts. Bake until the cake springs back when touched lightly in the center, or when a toothpick inserted in the center comes out clean, about 25 to 30 minutes.

Calhoun Coffee Cake

Makes one 9- by 13-inch cake

In 1901, Joseph Calhoun put ten dollars down on a 160-acre ranch off of Mines Road in the Livermore hills. On the ranch stood a wood-frame building said to have housed the driver of the horse-drawn stage that traveled from the Livermore train depot to Mendenhall Springs, about a ten mile distance. People from the "city" traveled to the Springs to "take the waters." In 1927, two years after his wife died, Joseph left San Leandro to live at the ranch. Here he raised sheep until his death. Today his granddaughter, Noel, lives in the ranch house. Noel is my husband Wayne's cousin and was my roommate at college. On Christmas Day, Noel holds an open house for members of the Calhoun family. The old ranch house has also been the location of many family reunions and parties. In the spring, family members tramp through hills to enjoy the wildflowers. The Calhoun coffeecake is served at many of the events. This recipe was given to the Calhouns by their Mines Road neighbor, May Cole.

MERILYN "TILLI" HOLM CALHOUN

Butter for oiling the pan
2 cups all-purpose flour plus more for dusting the pan
2 cups brown sugar
½ cup granulated sugar
¼ teaspoon salt
½ cup salad oil
2 teaspoons ground cinnamon
1 cup chopped nuts
1 egg, beaten
1 teaspoon baking powder
1 teaspoon baking soda
1¼ cups buttermilk

Preheat the oven to 350°F. Butter and flour a 9- by 13-inch pan.

In a bowl, thoroughly combine the flour, sugars, salt, and oil.

Put ¾ cup of the mixture in a small bowl and combine it with 1 teaspoon of the cinnamon and ½ cup of the chopped nuts. Set aside to use as a topping.

To the remaining mixture, add the egg, baking powder, baking soda, the remaining teaspoon cinnamon and buttermilk. Mix well and stir in the remaining ½ cup chopped nuts. Pour the batter into the pan, sprinkle with the topping, and bake for 40 minutes or until a toothpick inserted into the middle comes out clean. Cool before serving.

Calhoun Ranch on Mines Road
Noel Watson, Mike Calhoun, Joan Knoblich,
Wayne Calhoun, Jean Johnson, Bob Brown,
Sylvia Calhoun, Dale Brown, Chet Knoblich

Coffee Cake

Makes one 8-cup (10-inch) Bundt cake or two 6-cup (8-inch) Bundt cakes

I often use 2 small Bundt pans, which fit well in one-gallon freezer bags. This cake freezes well and is easy to take to family gatherings. I have also given it to friends as a Christmas morning gift.

Vicki Zabala Calhoun

½ cup oil plus more for oiling the pan
1 box yellow cake mix
1 (3.4-ounce) box instant vanilla pudding
4 eggs
1 cup sour cream
1 cup chopped walnuts
¾ cup sugar
2 tablespoons ground cinnamon

Preheat the oven to 350°F. Oil the Bundt pan.

Put the cake mix, pudding mix, oil, eggs, and sour cream in the bowl of an electric mixer. Mix at medium speed for about 3 minutes. In a separate small bowl, combine the walnuts, sugar, and cinnamon. Sprinkle ⅓ of the walnut mixture into the Bundt pan. Add ⅓ of the batter, another ⅓ of the walnut mixture, repeating until you've used all of the walnut mixture and batter. With a knife, cut through the batter three times.

Bake the 8-cup Bundt cake for about 1 hour. Two 6-cup cakes will take 35 to 40 minutes. The cake is done when a knife slipped into the center comes out clean.

Lemon Lust Dessert

Makes one 9- by 13-inch cake

Stanley and Edna Jorgensen

2 (3.4-ounce) packages instant lemon pudding
1 cup butter, melted plus more for oiling the pan
1¼ cups all-purpose flour
½ cup chopped walnuts
8 ounces cream cheese
1 cup powdered sugar
8 ounces Cool Whip
1 tablespoon grated lemon zest

Prepare the pudding using milk instead of water.

Preheat the oven to 350°F and butter a 9- by 13-inch baking pan.

In a small bowl, combine the butter, flour, and nuts. Press the mixture into the bottom of the pan. Place in the oven and bake for 15 minutes. Cool.

In a bowl, cream together the cream cheese and powdered sugar. Fold in half of the Cool Whip. Spread the cream cheese mixture on the cooled nut-butter layer in the baking pan. Evenly spread the pudding over the cream cheese layer. Spread the remaining Cool Whip on top. Garnish with the lemon zest. Chill for 3 hours before serving. To serve, cut into equal size squares.

Luscious Lemon Cheesecake *Makes one 9-inch cake, or 10 servings*

KATHIE GEORGE

Crust
2 cups crushed cinnamon graham
   crackers (about 26 crackers)
6 tablespoons unsalted butter, melted

Filling
3 (8-ounce) packages cream cheese,
   at room temperature
1⅓ cups sugar
3 eggs, at room temperature
¼ cup freshly squeezed lemon juice
1 tablespoon grated lemon zest
2 teaspoons vanilla extract

Topping
2 cups sour cream
3 tablespoons sugar
1 teaspoon vanilla extract

Glaze
¾ cup water
⅓ cup freshly squeezed lemon juice
1 egg yolk
½ cup sugar
1½ tablespoons cornstarch
¼ teaspoon salt
1 tablespoon butter
2 teaspoons grated lemon zest
Thinly sliced lemon rounds, halved
   and twisted

Preheat the oven to 350°F and butter a 9-inch springform pan.

To prepare the crust, blend the crumbs and melted butter in bowl. Press the mixture into the bottom and up the sides of the prepared pan. Bake 5 minutes. Cool.

To prepare the filling, place the cream cheese into the bowl of an electric stand mixer, and beat until soft. Gradually beat in the sugar. Beat in the eggs, 1 at a time. Add the lemon juice, lemon zest and vanilla and mix until thoroughly blended. Pour the filling into the crust and bake until slightly puffed, about 40 minutes.

To prepare the topping, combine the sour cream, sugar, and vanilla in a small bowl. Blend thoroughly. Spread on top of the cake and return to the oven. Bake for 15 minutes; the topping will not look set. Remove from the oven and cool for 30 minutes.

To prepare the glaze, combine the water, lemon juice and egg yolk in a small, heavy saucepan. Stir in the sugar, cornstarch, and salt. Bring to a boil over low heat, stirring constantly, about 10 minutes. Add the butter and lemon zest and stir until the butter melts. Cool the glaze for 20 minutes, then pour over the cake. Cool completely and refrigerate until well chilled.

Serve cold, garnished with lemon slices.

Persimmon Pudding

I always remember a flurry of activity on Christmas morning as Reba prepared the Christmas pudding to take to Ione's house. She steamed the pudding, which made the kitchen so warm and cozy. This recipe is baked in the oven, but if you want to steam it as Reba did, pour the pudding mixture into a well-buttered pudding mold with a tight-fitting lid. Place the mold on a trivet in a large, heavy pot with about an inch of water in the bottom. This pot should have a tight-fitting lid, as well. Bring the water to a boil, reduce the heat, and steam the pudding for about an hour. To make the persimmon pulp, push the persimmons through a sieve or colander. We like to serve this pudding with hard sauce.

Sue Kilgo Boies *recipe given to her by Reba Teeter Kilgo*

Reba and Bill
Kilgo

½ cup melted butter, plus more for oiling the baking dish

2 cups persimmon pulp (from about 4 to 6 ripe persimmons, depending on size)

1¼ cups sugar

1½ cups flour

1 teaspoon baking powder

1 teaspoon baking soda

½ teaspoon salt

3 eggs

2½ cups milk

2 teaspoons ground cinnamon

1 teaspoon ground ginger

½ teaspoon freshly grated nutmeg

½ cup golden raisins

½ cup chopped walnuts or pecans

Preheat the oven to 325°F, and butter a 2½-quart baking dish.

Put the persimmon pulp in a mixing bowl. In another bowl, combine the sugar, flour, baking powder, soda and salt. Beat the eggs into the pulp, then add the flour mixture, the melted butter, milk, cinnamon, ginger, and nutmeg. Fold in the raisins and nuts. Pour the mixture into the baking dish and bake in the oven until firm, about 1 hour.

Reba Teeter Kilgo

While attending Livermore High School, Ione's friends included Genevieve Smallwood (Frasier) and schoolmates from Pleasanton. One of Ione's favorite teachers, Bess Monahan (Wente), her home economics teacher, assisted her in making a red dress for the prom. Bess also took her students on many an outing.

In March of 1926, Ione was married to Warner (Dick) Holm at her Aunt Dixie's home in Alameda, where the Dan Teeter family was living. This began a partnership that lasted sixty years. Their attendants were Donna and Raymond Henry. Raymond took his brother Al's place as best man because Al had to work that day. After a Southern California honeymoon, the newlyweds set up housekeeping in an apartment in the Victorian house on the Holms' farm, Fair View, on the Livermore-Pleasanton Road. Ione married into a large Danish family. She became accustomed to Grandma Holm's Danish cooking and going to Dania Hall where their large family gathered for many holidays, weddings, and events. In the small house on the farm lived Leslie and Mona Holm with their sons Leslie and Bob, part of the extended Holm family. Dick and Leslie purchased a ranch on Mines Road and started their cattle business. New neighbors moved onto the farm, sister-in-law Gladys, Ben Benthien, and young Carl. All were included in many of the family activities.

In April of 1929, Dick and Ione were expecting their first child and were surprised when two were born, first Merilyn, and four minutes later, Frank. When Dick (a great tease) called with the news, nobody believed him because it was April Fool's Day. (Thirteen years later, his niece, Verda George, delivered twin girls on April 1.) In 1933, son James was born, followed by Richard in 1935 and Patricia in 1936. These were called the "Depression years." The banks closed when James was born, and the hospital had to wait for payments until the bank reopened.

Ione and Dick would entertain their friends Eleanor and Ray Henry. Eleanor recalled how delicious Ione's egg sandwiches were. Some Saturdays Dick would take the twins and Grandma Holm to the movies at the State Theater, where dishes were awarded as prizes.

Ione would pack up the kids and her "cowboy beans" in a cast-iron pot wrapped in newspapers, and she'd drive up Mines Road to the Circle H ranch for roundups and brandings. In the summer she would take the kids and some of their friends, along with clothes, bedding, food, and sometimes a milk cow, for a stay at the cabin to fix fences and haul rocks. She purchased groceries at Lou Gardella's Del Valle Mercantile, where the Holms had a running tab.

Ione and Dick loved the rodeo and the parade, which Ione attended for the last time in her wheelchair in 1997. When the children were young, on Saturdays the rodeo was free for children when accompanied by an adult. Ione would take her children and their friends.

Leslie Holm Jr. married Lois Hansen and moved into the "Little House" at Fair View. Sons Tommy and Bobby soon found their way to Ione's for cookies.

In July 1950, Merilyn married Wayne Calhoun; the reception held at the Holm farm. In August, Frank married Joan Voerckel, and by now, Ione could hardly wait to get her hands on a grandchild. Her first, Gary, was born in Tennessee (as was Dan Teeter), where Frank was stationed. Dick and Ione drove to Tennessee to see their new grandson. Patsy married Hank Neely in 1954, and they also held their reception at the farm. James married Carol Mooney in 1957. They moved into the apartment in the farm's "Big House." As the children married, the families of the new in-laws were soon included in the many Holm events—Easter, Fourth of July, and Christmas Eve.

During the 1950s and early '60s many grandchildren were to follow Gary: Susan, Dave, Merry, Wendy, Peggy, Lori, Nancy, and Jimmy. In 1966, the Holm farm was sold, and Ione and Dick built a new home on Mines Road. Tony and Blanche George, who had helped Dick and Les run the ranch over the years, lived next door in the caretaker's house on the Circle H. For roundups and brandings, friends and family would volunteer: Gus Koopmann, Freddy Shepard, Dale Anderson, Chet Sandbeck, Louis Draghi, Stanley Jorgensen, Frank Correia, John Kiely and his sons John and Dennis, Les, Lowell, and Bobby Holm, Frank, James, Richie Holm, Wayne Calhoun, and along with

Gladys Benthien, Grace Gardella and Ione at the Circle H swimming pool

Papa's real "cowboys," the grandchildren. In Granny and Papa's partnership, he ran the farm and ranch while she cooked for this wild crew (we all remember her famous "cowboy beans") and kept the books.

Dick and Ione now had time to travel, and they took trips to Alaska, Hawaii, Australia, New Zealand, and the Fiji Islands. They also went to Denmark, Holland, and Sweden with the McCumbers and Creight and Margaret Baxter. Many of the trips were planned through the Farm Bureau, giving them the opportunity to visit with other farmers from around the world. The grandchildren always looked forward to their postcards from across the globe, and especially to their return, with their suitcases brimming with souvenirs.

Many entertaining opportunities were celebrated. They were fêted on their fortieth anniversary with a party for family and friends. They enjoyed afternoon coffee with Phyllis Fachner and Stanley and Edna Jorgensen. The big event was the annual Christmas Eve

Sisters Ione Holm and Reba Kilgo enjoy a visit

lunch with the **entire** family—around ninety! Other parties included New Year's Eve plus many wedding rehearsals, weddings and baby showers, birthdays, and more. Dick and Ione celebrated their fiftieth anniversary at Shannon Park in Dublin (California). Family and friends filled Dania Hall for Dick's eighty-fifth birthday, and in 1986, the family gathered for Dick and Ione's sixtieth anniversary at the Dublin Corral owned by family friend Ed Packard. Dick passed away shortly after.

Tiramisu

Kristine Diltz Cataldo

3 egg yolks

3 tablespoons superfine sugar

¼ cup brandy or marsala

1 cup very strong espresso coffee, cooled

8 ounces mascarpone cheese, at room temperature

1 cup heavy whipping cream

3 egg whites

25 to 35 ladyfingers (about a 14-ounce package)

Cocoa powder or chocolate shavings, for garnish

Ron and Kristine Cataldo

Bring the water in the bottom of a double boiler to a boil; reduce the heat to low. In the top, beat together the egg yolks and sugar until ivory-colored. Whisk in the liquor and continue to stir over gently simmering water until thickened; let cool.

In a small bowl, stir ½ cup of the espresso into the mascarpone cheese; set aside.

Pour the cream into a bowl and whip to soft peaks; set aside.

In another bowl, beat the egg whites until stiff and fold into the egg mixture.

Pour the remaining ½ cup espresso into a shallow dish. Lightly dip the ladyfingers into the espresso; do not let them get soggy. Arrange the ladyfingers in a single layer in the bottom of an 8- by 8-inch glass baking dish. The number of ladyfingers needed will depend on the size of your ladyfingers.

Cover the ladyfingers with half of the mascarpone mixture. On top of this layer, spread half of the egg mixture. Follow with a layer of half of the whipped cream. Starting again by dipping the remaining ladyfingers in the coffee, repeat making the layers, using the remainder of the mascarpone, eggs, and whipped cream mixtures.

Refrigerate for several hours, or overnight. Garnish with the cocoa or chocolate shavings, as desired.

Raspberry Trifle

I make this trifle in a clear deep glass bowl that is about 9 inches in diameter and 6 inches deep.

SANDIE GEORGE LANDERS

1 (3-ounce) package of regular vanilla
    pudding (not instant)
2 cups half-and-half
1 to 2 tablespoons dark rum or
    1 teaspoon rum flavoring
1 pound cake
1 cup heavy whipping cream
1 teaspoon vanilla extract
3 tablespoons sugar
1 (10-ounce) jar raspberry jam
½ cup cream sherry
1 (10-ounce) package frozen raspberries,
    thawed

Topping
1 cup heavy whipping cream
1 teaspoon vanilla extract
3 to 4 tablespoons sugar
Fresh raspberries or slivered almonds,
    for garnish (optional)

Make the pudding according to the package instructions, using the half-and-half and rum in place of the milk. Chill the pudding thoroughly.

When the pudding is chilled, cut the cake into 3 layers, horizontally. Cut each layer into 1-inch cubes, keeping each layer separate.

Whip 1 cup of the heavy cream, beat in the vanilla and sugar. Fold the whipped cream into the chilled pudding.

To assemble the trifle, spread the sides of a 9-inch round clear glass bowl with some of the jam. Put the cubes from 1 cake layer into the bowl. Spread jam on each square and sprinkle ⅓ of the sherry over the cake squares. Add a layer of raspberries followed by a layer of pudding. Continue adding layers in this order: cake squares with jam, sherry, raspberries, and pudding. Be sure to spread the bottom of each cake square with jam before adding. Repeat as many times as you can, making 2 or 3 layers.

To make the topping, whip the cream with the vanilla and sugar to taste. Spread the whipped cream on the top of the trifle. Garnish with fresh berries or slivered almonds, if desired.

Chill the trifle for a couple of hours before serving.

Trifle

KATHIE GEORGE

Raspberry sauce

2 (10–ounce) packages frozen
　　raspberries, thawed
½ cup sugar
2 tablespoons cornstarch
¼ teaspoon salt
½ cup sweet red wine, such as port
2 tablespoons freshly squeezed
　　lemon juice

Quick custard

2 (3.75-ounce) packages instant vanilla
　　pudding mix
2 cups sour cream
2 cups milk

2 (10-ounce) angel food cake loaves,
　　sliced into 1-inch slices
3 to 4 tablespoons rum or brandy
1 cup heavy whipping cream
Powdered sugar
1 teaspoon vanilla extract
Slivered almonds, for garnish

To make the raspberry sauce, place the raspberries, with their juices, in a food processor fitted with the steel blade, or in a blender. Process until puréed. You can pour the mixture through a coarse strainer to remove the seeds, but it isn't necessary. In a small mixing bowl, mix the sugar, cornstarch, and salt completely so there are no lumps. Slowly add the wine and lemon juice, stirring well so the dry ingredients dissolve. Combine the raspberry purée and the sugar mixture in a saucepan. Cook over medium heat, stirring often, until the mixture thickens and becomes clear. Remove from the heat, pour into a bowl, and cover with plastic wrap or waxed paper so that the paper is touching the surface of the sauce. This prevents a skin from forming on the sauce. Chill until completely cold.

To make the custard, combine the pudding, sour cream, and milk in a deep bowl, and beat with an electric mixer until thick and creamy.

To assemble the dessert, place the cake slices in a single layer on a sheet of waxed paper. Sprinkle both sides of the slices with rum or brandy. The best way to do this is to pour the liquor into a clean spray bottle and spray each slice lightly. This will keep the cake from becoming soggy. Let the liquor soak into the cake for 15 minutes. Cut each slice into 3 pieces, each about 1- by 1- by 3-inches. Line the bottom of a 3-quart bowl (a trifle bowl is perfect, but any straight-sided, clear bowl will work) with the cake slices, making sure the entire surface of the bowl is covered. (You will have to cut some of the pieces in half, on a diagonal, to fit.) Spread ¼ to ⅓ of the custard over the cake, top with some of the chilled raspberry sauce, and continue to layer in this sequence (cake, custard, raspberry sauce), ending with the cake. Depending on the size of your bowl, you will have 3 or 4 layers. Cover and chill for 2 to 3 hours so the flavors will blend. Just before serving, whip the cream until stiff, flavor to taste with the sugar and vanilla, or a small amount of rum or brandy. Spread the whipped cream on top of the trifle. If desired, drizzle a small amount of the raspberry purée over the whipped cream, or top with sliced almonds or several whole raspberries. Serve immediately.

Granny's Tapioca Pudding

Makes 24 (½ cup) servings

Granny would make a huge bowl of this pudding to serve as Warren Howe's "birthday cake." She served it with strawberries.

Ione Teeter Holm

4 eggs, separated
1½ cups sugar
¾ cup small, quick-cooking pearl tapioca
8 cups milk
4 teaspoons vanilla extract
Fresh strawberries, for garnish

In a bowl, beat the egg whites until foamy. Gradually add ¾ cup of the sugar, beating until soft peaks form.

In a large saucepan, mix together the tapioca, the remaining sugar, milk, and egg yolks. Let stand for 5 minutes. Cook on medium heat, stirring constantly, until the mixture comes to a full boil.

Remove from the heat, cool slightly, and gently fold the egg whites into the tapioca mixture until well blended. Stir in the vanilla; chill for 20 minutes. Garnish with fresh strawberries.

Granny and Warren Howe with a huge bowl of tapioca pudding!

Livermore Dania Lodge

The Livermore Danish Lodge, Dannevang No. 7, for men, was organized in 1892. This was one of the Society Dania of California Lodges formed to preserve the language and customs of Denmark. It also provided assistance to fellow Danish immigrants. The Grand Lodge was formed to oversee the twenty-eight lodges throughout California and Nevada. Carl Holm was president of the Grand Lodge in 1908. In 1905 the Danebod, No. 16, was formed for women.

Through the generations, members of the Holm family joined both the Dannevang and Danebod. Many have enjoyed the annual Christmas party, the Frikadeller dinners, luncheons, and card parties through the years. The Dania Hall, located on Second Street in Livermore, has been host to Holm family events. Nancy and Bob Mueller's wedding reception, Dick Holm's eighty-fifth birthday party, Brett Rasmussen's and Ione Holm's funeral receptions were some of the family gatherings that took place at the hall.

Snee (Snow Pudding)

Serves 8

This recipe is shared by Paulette McCune Thomsen, daughter-in-law of Sigrid and Ruth Thomsen. Sigrid and Ruth were fellow Danish farmers in Pleasanton. The Thomsen family has always been very involved in the Dania Lodge, with several generations attending the annual Christmas party. Ruth Thomsen served as Grand President of the Grand Lodge of Dannebrog in 1981, and her daughter Kathy Thomsen Reinstein, served in 2008. Snee is the Thomsens' traditional Christmas Eve dessert. Paulette hides an almond in it, and the person who finds it gets a prize. "I hope you enjoy it. Making it is always a challenge."

SUSIE CALHOUN

Pudding
1 tablespoon unflavored gelatin
¼ cup cold water
¾ cup boiling water
1 cup sugar
⅓ cup freshly squeezed lemon juice
3 egg whites

Custard sauce
3 cups milk
3 eggs
⅛ cup sugar
Pinch of salt
1 teaspoon vanilla extract

To make the pudding, soak the gelatin in the water for 5 minutes in the bowl of an electric mixer. Add the boiling water and stir to dissolve the gelatin. Stir in the sugar and lemon juice. Allow to cool, stirring occasionally. When quite thick, beat with the mixer until foamy. In a separate bowl, using a whisk or clean beaters, beat the egg whites until stiff. Add the egg whites to the gelatin mixture and continue beating until the mixture holds its shape. This requires a lot of beating—maybe as long as 30 minutes. Pour the mixture into a 1½ to 2-quart bowl and refrigerate until chilled, approximately 2 hours.

To make the custard sauce, scald the milk in a double boiler. In a small bowl, beat the eggs lightly and add the sugar and salt. Gradually pour the egg mixture into the scalded milk, whisking constantly. Cook in the double boiler, stirring constantly, until the mixture thickens enough to coat the back of a spoon. Cool, then stir in the vanilla.

Spoon the pudding into individual bowls and serve with custard sauce.

Cowboy Cookies

Makes 5 dozen cookies

I received this recipe several years ago from my good friend Gayle Koopmann McLelland. The Koopmann family has been ranching in Sunol for four generations.

Merry "Lambie" Calhoun Carter

1 cup sugar
1 cup packed brown sugar
1 cup shortening
2 eggs
2 cups sifted flour
1 teaspoon baking soda
½ teaspoon baking powder
½ teaspoon salt
1 teaspoon vanilla
2 cups rolled oats
1 (12-ounce) package chocolate chips

Preheat the oven to 350°F. In a bowl, cream together both sugars and the shortening. Add the eggs and blend well. In another bowl, combine the flour, soda, baking powder, and salt. Add the flour mixture to the creamed sugar and mix well. Add the vanilla. When all the ingredients are well blended, add the oats and chocolate chips. Drop tablespoon-size balls about 2 inches apart onto ungreased cookie sheets. Bake for 15 minutes or until golden brown.

Cousin Charlotte Koch Hvilsted of Denmark visits with Granny and twins Drew and Loren Holm

M&M Cookies

Makes about 6 dozen cookies

Susie Calhoun

1 cup vegetable shortening
1 cup firmly packed brown sugar
½ cup sugar
2 eggs
2 teaspoons vanilla extract
2¼ cups sifted flour
1 teaspoon baking soda
1 teaspoon salt
¾ pound bag M&M's

Preheat the oven to 375°F.

In a bowl, cream the shortening, both sugars, eggs, and vanilla thoroughly. In another bowl, sift together the flour, soda, and salt. Add the dry ingredients and ½ cup M&M's to the shortening mixture. Blend well. Drop spoonfuls of dough onto an ungreased cookie sheet. Slightly push the remaining M&M's into the tops of the cookies, and bake for 10 to 12 minutes, or until golden brown.

Chocolate Angel Fancy

Serves 8 to 12

This recipe calls for raw egg whites that remain uncooked. If you prefer, you can use meringue powder, which can be purchased at stores that sell cake decorating supplies. Follow the directions on the can for preparation. The size of the angel food cake used really doesn't matter—it can be an 8-, 9-, or 10-inch cake.

DOROTHY TEETER

2 (6.5-ounce) packages semisweet
    chocolate pieces

2 tablespoons water

3 egg yolks, beaten together

1 teaspoon vanilla extract

½ teaspoon salt

1 tablespoon sugar

1 cup heavy cream, whipped, plus more
    for garnish

3 stiffly beaten egg whites

1 angel food cake, broken into pieces

In a double boiler, over medium heat, add the chocolate pieces and water and melt together. Blend in the egg yolks; cook and stir for about 1 minute. Stir in the vanilla and salt. Cool.

In another bowl, fold the sugar into the whipped cream; then fold this cream into the chocolate mixture. Fold the egg whites into the chocolate-cream mixture. Place the broken cake pieces in a 9- by 13- by 2-inch dish. Pour the chocolate-cream mixture over the cake. Chill for several hours or overnight. To serve, cut into squares and top with a dollop of whipped cream.

Remembering Ione

Granny was a remarkable woman. When I "Google" the string of text "attributes of a remarkable woman," the words courage, faith, love, and humility were found. Add to that list resourceful and influential, and there you have her—Granny. She was a courageous woman who faced hardships in life that made her stronger and developed her strong value of family. And she was the only ninety-year-old woman I know who killed a rattlesnake by whacking it with a shovel. Unconditional love of family was her priority. To Granny, family did not just consist of blood relatives; the friends and in-laws of her children and grandchildren considered her their mom or their "Granny," too. She was not wealthy in the fiscal sense, but her resourcefulness and character made her a very rich woman. She influenced people by making them feel right at home just moments after entering her house, and she influenced her family to work hard, to become upstanding adults—people with integrity. It is very unfortunate that not all families have a Granny in their lives.

—Merry Carter, granddaughter

Oatmeal Crisps

IONE TEETER HOLM

½ cup vegetable shortening (Crisco)
½ cup (1 stick) butter
1 cup brown sugar
1 cup granulated sugar
2 eggs
1½ cups flour
1 teaspoon salt
1 teaspoon baking soda
3 cups rolled oats
1 teaspoon vanilla extract
¾ cups chopped nuts

In a bowl, cream together the shortening, butter, and both sugars. Add the eggs and mix well. In a separate bowl, combine the flour, salt, baking soda, and oats. Add the dry ingredients into the creamed mixture. Blend thoroughly. Add the vanilla and nuts. Mix well. Pack the dough into a waxed paper-lined old-fashioned aluminum ice cube tray or shape into a 4- by 1½- by 10-inch loaf. Leave in the refrigerator 2 hours or overnight.

When you are ready to bake the cookies, preheat the oven to 375°F. Turn the dough out of the ice cube tray, and slice into ¼-inch-thick pieces. The crisps will be about 4- by 1½- by ¼-inch. Place them 2 inches apart on an ungreased cookie sheet. Bake for 12 minutes, or until golden brown. Cool on the cookie sheet.

Nancy's Lemon Squares

Makes 12 squares

My cookbook fetish began in 1970 with my very first cookbook, The Peanuts Cookbook. *My favorite recipe was Lucy's Lemon Squares. This is my version.*

NANCY CALHOUN MUELLER

2 cups flour
½ cup powdered sugar plus more for
    sprinkling on top
1 cup (2 sticks) unsalted butter, chilled
4 eggs
2 cups granulated sugar
1 teaspoon baking powder
5 tablespoons freshly squeezed lemon juice
1 tablespoon lemon zest
Pinch of salt

Preheat the oven to 350°F.

In a bowl, sift together the flour and powdered sugar. Cut the butter into the flour mixture until it resembles coarse cornmeal. You can use a pastry blender, your fingertips, or a food processor. Pat the dough evenly into the bottom of a 8- by 8-inch baking dish. Bake for 20 minutes or until lightly golden.

Meanwhile, using an electric mixer, beat together the eggs, sugar, baking powder, juice, zest, and salt. Pour over the baked crust and return to the oven. Bake until the filling begins to brown at the edges and is just springy to the touch, about 20 to 25 minutes. Cool completely on a rack. Cut into squares and sprinkle with sifted powdered sugar.

Gingerbread Cookies

Makes 2 to 3 dozen cookies, depending on the size of your cookie cutter

I based this recipe on one I found while waiting for Thanksgiving dinner at the Ken Calhouns in Yuba City. It is tradition that we arrive early and have some appetizers while we browse through the Christmas catalogs and magazines. I was inspired by the cute faces on some gingerbread cookies that were featured in a local magazine. I took it a step further and made anatomically correct gingerbread people, mallard ducks, and Christmas trees.

SUSIE CALHOUN

½ cup vegetable shortening (Crisco)
½ cup sugar
½ cup molasses
1½ teaspoons distilled white vinegar
1 egg, beaten
3 cups flour
½ teaspoon baking soda
½ teaspoon ground cinnamon
½ teaspoon ground ginger

Glaze
1 egg white
1½ cups powdered sugar
Food coloring, if desired

To make the cookies, mix together the shortening, sugar, molasses, and vinegar in a large heavy saucepan. Bring the mixture to a boil, then let it cool. Mix in the egg. Into a bowl, sift together the flour, soda, cinnamon, and ginger. Add the molasses mixture. Mix well and chill at least 2 hours or until stiff.

When you are ready to bake the cookies, preheat the oven to 375˚F. Roll the dough out to ⅛-inch thick. Cut out shapes using your favorite cutters. Bake for 8 to 12 minutes or until lightly browned. Be careful, as they darken easily. Remove them from the oven and let them cool.

To make the glaze, mix together the egg white and powdered sugar. Add food coloring if desired. Apply the glaze to the cooled cookies with a small-tipped pastry tube.

Sophie's Danish Cookies

Makes about 6 dozen cookies

This is my favorite family cookie recipe, which comes from Sophie Jorgensen Holm. My mother, Tilli, would make these for Christmas. She would make the dough in advance, leaving it in the refrigerator for several days. I would sneak in and eat the raw dough. It was my favorite, cooked or raw!

SUSIE CALHOUN

1 cup granulated sugar

1 cup brown sugar

¾ cup vegetable shortening (Crisco)

¾ cup (1½ sticks) butter, plus more for buttering the cookie sheet

½ teaspoon baking soda, dissolved in ½ teaspoon water

3 eggs, beaten

4½ cups all-purpose flour

1 teaspoon cinnamon

½ teaspoon salt

1 cup chopped walnuts

In a bowl, cream together both sugars, shortening, butter, and dissolved baking soda. Stir in the eggs and mix until well blended. In a separate bowl, sift together the flour, cinnamon, and salt. Add the dry ingredients to the shortening mixture and mix well. Shape the dough into rolls, about 2½ to 3 inches in diameter and about 8 inches long. Wrap in waxed paper and chill for at least 2 hours, or until firm.

When you are ready to bake the cookies, preheat the oven to 350°F and butter a cookie sheet. Remove the dough from the waxed paper and cut it into ¼-inch slices. Place on the cookie sheet and bake for 10 minutes or until a light golden brown.

Original drawing of Art and Sophie Holm's house on South "L" Street. by Tilli Calhoun

Art and Sophie Holm's House 511 So L

Granny's Chocolate Chip Cookies
Makes 4 dozen cookies

IONE TEETER HOLM

1 cup vegetable shortening (Crisco),
    plus more to oil the pans
¾ cup granulated sugar
¾ cup firmly-packed brown sugar
2 eggs
½ teaspoon water
1 teaspoon vanilla extract
2¼ cups all-purpose flour
1 teaspoon baking soda
1 teaspoon salt
1 cup chopped walnuts
1 (12-ounce) package chocolate chips

Preheat the oven to 375°F and oil (or spray) several cookie sheets.

In a bowl, cream together the shortening and both sugars. Add the eggs, water, and vanilla and mix until well blended. In another bowl, combine the flour, baking soda, and salt. Add the dry ingredients to the creamed shortening mixture and mix thoroughly. Add the nuts and chocolate chips and mix again. Drop spoonfuls of the dough onto a cookie sheet and bake for 12 minutes or until light brown.

Rosettes
Makes 2 dozen cookies

This old-fashioned Scandinavian recipe is called Sockerstruvor in Swedish. This was an old family recipe given to me by Swedish 20/30 friend Shirley Bray. The rosettes are delicate "flowers" fried on a special iron in hot oil.

PATSY HOLM NEELY

2 eggs
1 tablespoon granulated sugar
¼ teaspoon salt
1 cup all-purpose flour
1 cup heavy cream
1 teaspoon vanilla
Vegetable shortening for frying
Powdered sugar

In a mixing bowl, combine the eggs, granulated sugar, and salt; beat well. Add the flour, cream, and vanilla and beat until smooth.

Place paper towels on a cooling rack. Heat a rosette iron in 2-inch-deep vegetable shortening which has been heated to 375°F. Dip the hot rosette iron into the batter, being careful that the batter only comes three quarters of the way up the side of the iron.

Fry the dough-dipped iron in the hot oil until golden, about ½ minute. Lift the iron out of the shortening and tip slightly to drain off any excess. With a fork, carefully push the rosette off the iron onto the paper towels. Reheat the iron and continue making rosettes. Sift powdered sugar over the cooled rosettes.

Russian Tea Cakes

Makes about 4 dozen tea cakes

JOHNNY GILDERSLEEVE

1 cup (2 sticks) butter
½ cup powdered sugar plus more for rolling the cookies
1 teaspoon vanilla extract
2¼ cups all-purpose flour
¼ teaspoon salt
¾ cup chopped nuts

Preheat the oven to 350°F. In a bowl, cream together the butter and sugar. Add the vanilla and blend well. In another bowl, sift together the flour and salt and add to the creamed mixture along with the nuts. Roll into 1-inch balls. Place them on an unbuttered cookie sheet. Bake until set but not brown, 8 to 10 minutes. When cool, roll the cakes in powdered sugar.

Shortcakes

Makes 6 cakes

IDA JESSEN HOLM

1½ cups all-purpose flour
2½ teaspoons baking powder
½ teaspoon salt
2 tablespoons sugar
½ cup vegetable shortening
1 egg, beaten
5 tablespoons milk

Preheat the oven to 450°F. In a bowl, combine the flour, baking powder, salt, and sugar. Add the shortening and blend together until the mixture resembles coarse cornmeal. Add the egg and milk and gently mix. Knead lightly 5 or 6 times to form into a ball. Divide the dough evenly into 6 pieces. Form each piece into a ball and flatten. Place the cakes on an unbuttered cookie sheet and bake for 15 to 20 minutes or until golden brown.

There are certain cookie recipes that have become perennial favorites at the Holm family Christmas lunch and other family gatherings. Among the tops are Aunt Sophie's refrigerator cookies, Granny's spritz, gingerbread, chocolate chip cookies, and Russian tea cakes.

Chocolate chip or Toll-House cookies originated on the East Coast in the 1930s, and when they made their way to California, they were a hit. At that time, chocolate chips were not available, so thick bars of chocolate were chopped into small chunks.

The Russian tea cake recipe came to our family in the 1940s when Johnny Gildersleeve invited friends of her daughter, Shirley, to her house for a cookie-making party. Shirley married Joe Regan, whose grandmother was one of the young Danish girls who stayed with Carl and Ida Holm when she emigrated from Denmark. Joe was the proprietor of Regan Christmas Trees in Livermore for over fifty years, and he now lives in Oregon.

Flan (Spanish custard)

Serves 8 to 9

SANDIE GEORGE LANDERS

1 cup plus ⅓ cup sugar
4 eggs plus 4 egg yolks
⅛ teaspoon salt
2½ cups milk, low-fat or whole
1 cup cream
1 teaspoon vanilla extract

Preheat the oven to 350°F. In a pan over medium heat, add 1 cup of the sugar and stir until lightly browned and melted, about 5 minutes. Pour into the bottom of an 8- or 9-inch baking dish and set aside. In a bowl, beat together the eggs and egg yolks well. Add the remaining ⅓ cup sugar and the salt. Scald the milk and cream in a small pot. Let it cool a bit; then slowly add it to the egg mixture, whisking constantly. Add the vanilla and pour the mixture into the dish over the hardened sugar glaze. Set the baking dish with the flan inside a larger baking dish and fill the larger dish with enough water to come halfway up the sides of the flan dish. Bake for 45 minutes or until the flan is set in the center. The cooking time will depend on the temperature of the water in the larger dish. It can range from 45 minutes to over an hour.

Chill the flan for several hours or overnight. When ready to serve, bring it to room temperature. Run a sharp knife around the edges, place a serving plate on top of the baking dish, and flip upside down. Gently remove the baking dish. Cut into 9 pieces and serve.

Caramel Crunch Popcorn

Makes 2 pounds

I make this at Christmas time and give to my family. It is a favorite with everyone.

PATSY HOLM NEELY

1 cup (2 sticks) butter or margarine plus more for buttering the pan
8 cups popped corn
1 cup pecan halves, toasted (see note)
1 cup whole, unblanched almonds, toasted (see note)
1⅓ cups sugar
½ cup light corn syrup
1 teaspoon vanilla extract

Butter a shallow baking pan, and combine the popped corn and nuts in it. In a saucepan, combine the sugar, butter, and corn syrup. Bring to a boil over medium heat, stirring constantly. Continue boiling, stirring occasionally, until the mixture turns a caramel color (hard-crack stage). Remove from the heat and stir in the vanilla. Pour the caramel over the popcorn-nut mixture and stir to coat well. Using 2 forks, separate the mixture into clusters. Store in a tightly closed bag or container.

Note: To toast the nuts, spread them on an unoiled baking sheet and bake in a 350°F oven for 8 to 10 minutes. Stir once or twice while toasting.

Granny's Apple Crumble

IONE TEETER HOLM

Serves 6

½ cup (1 stick) butter plus more for
    buttering the dish
4 medium apples, peeled and thinly sliced
Cinnamon
Sugar
1 cup flour
1 cup firmly packed brown sugar

Preheat the oven to 350°F and butter a square 8- by 8- by 2-inch casserole dish. Place the apples in the casserole dish and sprinkle with cinnamon and sugar to taste. In a bowl, combine the flour and brown sugar. Cut in the butter until the butter is in pea-size pieces. Cover the top of the apples evenly with the flour-butter mixture. Place in the oven and bake for 45 minutes, or until the apples are soft and the topping is browned.

Risengrad (Rice Pudding)

Serves 6 to 8

This is not only an excellent, satisfying, everyday dish, but it also appears on the menu of many a festive Danish Christmas dinner. "Christmas Eve, you are so sweet! Rice pudding shall be our treat!" sings the poet. The children gobble up their rice pudding as fast as they can, hoping to be the one to find the almond hidden in it and thereby win the traditional prize of a marzipan pig. Dick Holm had memories of looking for the prize in his rice pudding when he was a small boy.

MERILYN "TILLI" HOLM CALHOUN

2 quarts milk
1¾ cups white rice, rinsed and drained
Salt
Cold butter

Optional
Ground cinnamon
Sugar
Hot malt beer
Watered-down fruit juice

Put 2 tablespoons cold water in a pot over high heat and bring it to a boil. Pour in the milk and return it to a boil. Add the rice and stir continuously until it returns to a boil. Cover, reduce the heat, and let simmer for 1 hour or until thickened. Watch and stir the rice occasionally. You want the texture of the rice, so don't cook the pudding so long that the grains break down. Add salt to taste.

Serve with cold butter and your choice of optional additions.

Baumkuchen (Tree Cake)

Makes one 9- by 5- by 2¾-inch loaf

This cake is very popular in fancy bakeries in Germany. The name comes from it being baked in layers and in pans shaped like logs. In Germany, this cake is loved at Christmas time.

PETRA HILLGRUBER HOLM

1 cup (2 sticks) butter or margarine, at room temperature plus more for buttering
    the pan
6 eggs
1 cup sugar
1 teaspoon vanilla extract
3 tablespoons rum
1 cup flour
⅔ cup cornstarch
1½ teaspoons baking powder
1¼ cups powdered sugar
3 tablespoons soft butter or margarine
1 tablespoon unsweetened cocoa powder
3 tablespoons hot water

Preheat the oven to 400°F, place the rack at the lowest position. Butter well a 9¼- by 5¼- by 2¾-inch loaf pan. Separate 4 of the eggs and beat the egg whites until stiff.

In a large bowl, beat the butter until creamy. Add the sugar, vanilla, 2 whole eggs, the 4 egg yolks, and the rum, and beat until creamy. In a bowl, combine the flour, cornstarch, and baking powder and stir them into the egg mixture. Gently fold in the egg whites.

Spread 2 tablespoons of batter on the bottom of the loaf pan. Bake 6 to 7 minutes, or until golden brown. Take out of the oven and spread another 2 tablespoons of batter over the first layer; bake 6 to 7 minutes. Repeat until all the batter has been used; there should be at least 10 layers. After the last layer is baked, invert the cake onto a platter.

In a small bowl, combine the powdered sugar, butter, cocoa, and hot water. Blend thoroughly and spread over the cake.

The wedding of Jim Holm and
Petra Hillgruber, 1993.

Petra and Jim
Christmas, 2007

 # Sugared Walnuts

Sugared walnuts were a traditional treat at Christmas. Children who grow up on farms are assigned many chores. At Fair View, the annual walnut harvest involved the entire Holm family and sometimes friends. Brown fingers were evidence to schoolmates, identifying those who shared this chore, as fingers were stained brown from hulling the walnuts. Grandma Holm told of using the hulls to stain strands of gray hair brown. This sugared walnut recipe was passed down by Ida Holm to her daughter Mabel (May) Holm Jorgensen and daughter-in-law, Ione Teeter Holm. Janet Fachner said that her grandmother, May, also made this special treat for Christmas.

IONE TEETER HOLM

½ cup sour cream
½ cup white sugar
1 cup firmly packed brown sugar
1 teaspoon vanilla extract
2 quarts walnut halves

In a pot over medium heat, combine the sour cream, both sugars, and vanilla. Cook to the soft-ball stage (about 235°F on a candy thermometer) or until a soft ball forms when a bit of the mixture is dropped into cold water and flattens of its own accord when it is removed. Place the nuts in a large bowl, pour the sugar syrup over the walnuts, and stir well until all the walnuts are coated. Let the syrup harden, then break up the coated walnuts into bite-size chunks.

Swedish Walnuts

Serves 24, unless addicted!

These walnuts are addictive—it's easy to eat them all by yourself.

BECKY CALHOUN FOSTER

2 egg whites
1 cup sugar
3½ cups walnut halves
½ cup (1 stick) butter, melted

Preheat the oven to 300°F. In a bowl, beat the egg whites until stiff. Fold in the sugar. Stir in the walnuts and pour this mixture onto a jelly roll pan or cookie sheet. Evenly pour the melted butter over the walnut mixture.

Gently shake the pan to distribute the walnuts evenly, then bake for a total of 40 to 50 minutes, or until the nuts are golden brown. After the first 20 minutes, gently stir them to prevent burning. After this, stir every 10 minutes until done.

Pumpkin-Pecan Cheesecake

Makes one 9-inch cheesecake

This is the best cheesecake I have ever tasted—it's to die for!

BECKY CALHOUN FOSTER

Praline

½ cup packed light brown sugar
3 tablespoons unsalted butter
¾ cup coarsely chopped pecans

Crust

2 cups gingersnap cookie crumbs
1 teaspoon ground cinnamon
¼ cup (½ stick) unsalted butter, melted

Filling

4 (8-ounce) packages cream cheese,
    at room temperature
1½ cups sugar
3 tablespoons all-purpose flour
1½ teaspoons ground cinnamon
1 teaspoon ground ginger
4 large eggs
1 (15-ounce) can pumpkin
3 tablespoons bourbon
2 teaspoons vanilla extract

To make the praline, preheat the oven to 325°F. Line a baking sheet with foil. In a heavy medium-size saucepan over medium heat, combine the sugar and butter and stir until the sugar melts and the mixture comes to boil; boil for 1 minute without stirring. Mix in the pecans. Spread the mixture on the baking sheet and bake until the sugar syrup bubbles vigorously, about 8 minutes. Cool the praline completely. Break into pieces. (This can be made one day ahead. Store in an airtight container.)

To make the crust, preheat the oven to 325°F. In a bowl, combine the cookie crumbs and cinnamon. Add the butter and stir until the crumbs are evenly moistened. Press onto the bottom and 1 inch up the sides of 9-inch diameter springform pan with 2¾-inch sides. Bake the crust until it sets, about 8 minutes. Cool. Double-wrap the outside of pan with heavy-duty foil and place in a large roasting pan.

To make the filling, using an electric mixer, beat the cream cheese and sugar in a large bowl until smooth. Beat in the flour, cinnamon, and ginger. Beat in the eggs, one at a time. Beat in the pumpkin, bourbon, and vanilla. Pour into the crust.

Pour enough hot water into the roasting pan to reach 1 inch up the sides of the springform pan. With the oven still at 325°F, bake the cake in the water bath until the center is just set, about 1 hour and 45 minutes. Add more water to the roasting pan as needed. Remove the cheesecake from the water. Cool in the pan on a rack. Remove the foil; run a small sharp knife between the cake and the pan sides. Chill until cold; then cover and chill overnight.

To serve, release the pan sides and remove. Place the cake on a platter. Sprinkle the praline on the top, leaving a 1-inch plain border at the edge. Cut into wedges and serve.

Quarkkaesekuchen (German Cheesecake) *Makes one 10-inch cheese cake*

Quark is a soft, unripened cow's milk cheese with the texture and flavor of sour cream. You can buy it at farmers' markets.

PETRA HILLGRUBER HOLM

Bread crumbs, for lining cake form
2¼ pounds quark
¾ cup plus 2 tablespoons butter, softened
1 cup plus 1 tablespoon sugar
1 (⁵/₁₆-ounce) packet vanilla sugar
1 tablespoon lemon juice
5 eggs
¼ cup plus 3 tablespoons flour
1 tablespoon baking powder

Preheat the oven to 420°F. Butter a 9-inch springform cake pan and coat the sides with bread crumbs. Over a large bowl, press the quark through a medium mesh sieve. Add the butter to the quark and cream together thoroughly. Add the sugar to the mixture and blend. Add the vanilla sugar and blend together again. Add the lemon juice and mix again. Add the eggs, one at a time, blending each egg into the mixture before adding another. Add the flour and blend, and finally the baking powder. Mix to blend thoroughly. Pour into the cake form and bake for 60 to 70 minutes, or until the top is golden brown and an inserted toothpick comes out clean. Place on a rack to cool. After cooling, the cheesecake falls somewhat. Chill before serving.

Coconut Macaroons

Makes 5 dozen cookies

I am "double-Danish," as both sides of my family are Danish. Tilli Calhoun said she remembered my Gramma Bonde making these cookies when she was a little girl. She said the cookies were as big as her hand. My paternal grandparents, Hans and Nina Bonde, would come with the cookhouse and the five-wire baler and bale the Holm hay on Stanley Boulevard.

KIM BONDE

1 cup brown sugar
1 cup white sugar
1 cup (2 sticks) butter or shortening, melted
1 cup sweetened flaked coconut
2 eggs, beaten
1 teaspoon vanilla extract
1 cup flour
½ teaspoon salt
¾ teaspoon baking soda
4 cups rolled oats (such as Quaker oats)

Preheat the oven to 350°F. In a bowl, blend the sugars and the butter. Mix in the coconut, eggs, and vanilla and stir well. Add the flour, salt, baking soda, and oats, and mix until well blended. Shape into 1-inch balls by hand. Place on an ungreased cookie sheet and press each ball flat with the bottom of a glass (dip the bottom of the glass in sugar if the dough sticks). Bake for 15 minutes or until golden brown. Let cool for 3 minutes before removing from the sheet.

Nina and Hans Bonde

Patsy's Cherry Cheesecake

Makes one 9-inch cheesecake

Patsy Holm Neely

Graham cracker crust

1½ cups fine graham cracker crumbs
    (about 24 crackers)
⅓ cup butter or margarine, melted
¼ cup sugar

Cheesecake

3 (8-ounce) packages cream cheese,
    softened
½ teaspoon salt
1 tablespoon vanilla extract
4 eggs, at room temperature
1 cup plus 2 tablespoons sugar
1 pint (2 cups) sour cream

Topping

1 (21-ounce) can cherry pie filling
2 tablespoons kirsch (or cherry brandy)

Preheat the oven to 350°F.

To make the crust, combine the graham cracker crumbs, butter, and sugar in a bowl. Press the mixture firmly into the bottom and 2 inches up the sides of a 9-inch spring-form pan. Bake for 10 minutes. Set aside to cool.

In a large bowl, blend together the cream cheese, salt, and vanilla until soft and creamy. Add the eggs, 1 at a time, and beat well after each addition. Gradually beat in the 1 cup sugar until it is all incorporated. Pour into the prepared pan.

Bake for 30 to 35 minutes or until the center jiggles slightly when the pan is gently shaken (the center will set upon cooling). Remove the cake from the oven and let stand for 20 minutes.

Increase the oven temperature to 450°F. In a small bowl, stir together the sour cream and the 2 tablespoons sugar; spread gently over the top of the cake. Return the cake to the oven and bake for 5 more minutes or until the cream is set. Transfer the pan to a wire rack and let cool completely before removing the sides from the pan. Cover and refrigerate for at least 24 hours.

When you are ready to serve, mix the cherry pie filling with the kirsch and spoon it onto the top of the cheesecake.

Gingerbread Boys

IONE TEETER HOLM

⅔ cup shortening (Crisco), at
    room temperature

½ cup sugar

½ cup molasses

1 egg, beaten

3 cups all-purpose flour

½ teaspoon salt

1 teaspoon baking powder

1 teaspoon baking soda

1 teaspoon ground cinnamon

1 teaspoon ground cloves

1 teaspoon ground ginger

½ teaspoon grated nutmeg

In a bowl, cream together the shortening, sugar, and molasses. Add the egg and blend well. In another bowl, sift together the flour, salt, baking powder, baking soda, cinnamon, cloves, ginger, and nutmeg. Add to the shortening mixture. Chill several hours or overnight.

When ready to bake, preheat the oven to 350°F and oil a baking sheet.

On a floured board, roll out the dough to ¼ inch thick and cut into the desired shapes. Place on the cookie sheet and bake for 8 to 10 minutes.

Mimi's Peanut Brittle

Serves 12

My mother used to give this as Christmas gifts. Getting the temperature exactly right for the candy to harden is an art, but she did a great job. Her brittle would melt in your mouth. I recommend using raw Spanish peanuts, which you can find at health food stores.

CAROL HOLM NEWMAN

Butter for oiling the pan

2 cups sugar

1 cup light corn syrup

½ cup hot water

Pinch of salt

2½ cups raw peanuts

2 teaspoons baking soda

1 teaspoon vanilla extract

Butter a 14- by 20-inch baking sheet.

In a saucepan, combine the sugar, corn syrup, hot water, and salt and mix well. Cook over high heat until the mixture reaches 300°F or the hard-crack stage. Add the raw peanuts to the mixture and cook on medium-high until it turns soft yellow, stirring constantly. Be careful to keep the mixture at 300°F. Stir in the baking soda and vanilla. Turn out onto the baking sheet and spread the brittle into a thin sheet. When cool, break it into pieces and store in an air-tight container.

Poor Man's Cookies

These cookies got their name during the depression when eggs and butter were not readily available. During our recipe testing, these cookies came out best when made using margarine. However, the original recipe called for ½ cup of oil or vegetable shortening.

VERNA FACHNER SAXTON

½ cup margarine plus more for oiling the
    baking sheets
2 cups rolled oats (such as Quaker oats)
1 cup packed brown sugar
½ cup sugar
1 cup all-purpose flour
¼ teaspoon salt
1 teaspoon baking soda
¼ cup hot water
1 teaspoon vanilla extract
⅓ cup chopped walnuts

Preheat the oven to 350°F and butter 2 cookie sheets.

In a mixing bowl, combine the oats, sugars, flour, and salt. In a small bowl, combine the baking soda and water; stir into the oat mixture. Add the margarine, vanilla, and walnuts and mix well. Roll the dough into walnut-size balls and place on the cookie sheets 2 inches apart. Bake for about 10 minutes or until golden brown. Remove from the oven; allow to stand 2 minutes before moving the cookies to a wire rack to cool.

*Verna Fachner Saxton
and Patsy Holm*

Amaretto Squares

PHYLLIS JORGENSEN FACHNER

1 cup (2 sticks) butter, softened
    (½ can be margarine)
1 cup sugar
1 egg, separated
2 teaspoons finely grated orange zest
1½ tablespoons amaretto
¼ teaspoon salt
2 cups all-purpose flour
¾ cup sliced almonds

Preheat the oven to 300°F. In a mixing bowl, beat the butter and sugar until creamy. Add the egg yolk and beat well. Stir in the orange zest, amaretto, and salt. Add the flour and blend well. Evenly line the bottom of an unbuttered 15- by 10- by 1-inch jelly roll pan with the dough, pressing it out with your fingers.

In a clean bowl, beat the egg white until foamy. Spread it over the dough and sprinkle with the almonds. Bake for 45 minutes or until brown. Remove from the oven and cut into squares while warm.

Streuselkuchen (Streusel Cake)

Makes one 15- by 10-inch cake

In Germany this cake is often served at funerals.

Petra Hillgruber Holm

Cake

2⅓ cups all-purpose flour
2 teaspoons baking powder
⅓ cup sugar
1 egg
5 tablespoons ricotta cheese
5 tablespoons butter or margarine, cut into ½-inch pieces
1 cup raisins

Streusel topping

2⅓ cups flour
½ teaspoon baking powder
⅔ cup sugar
11 tablespoons butter or margarine

Preheat the oven to 375°F.

To make the cake, pour the flour on the counter top and sprinkle the baking powder and sugar over it. Make a well in the middle of the flour and drop in the egg and the ricotta cheese. Sprinkle the butter pieces and raisins on top. Carefully work the flour and other ingredients together and knead into a smooth dough. Roll out the dough and line a 15- by 10- by 1-inch baking pan with it.

To make the streusel, combine the flour, baking powder, and sugar in a bowl. Slice the butter over the flour. Mix the butter with a fork into the flour mixture. The butter will be in fairly big chunks. Sprinkle the streusel topping over the cake dough and bake in the oven for 25 to 30 minutes, or until light brown.

Remembering
Granny and Papa

Of all the places that I recall,
the ranch is certainly the best of all.

It is the one place where I feel the
most secure,
and have learned to value what
is dear.

For it was the loving and wise ways
of Papa and Granny,
who taught me that above all we
value family.

To cherish our traditions
and value each other in all kinds
of conditions.
I learned that with joy must come
sorrow,
and yet they helped instill in me
an unshakable faith in tomorrow.

— *Peggy Rennick,*
granddaughter

Skillet Coconut Cookies

Makes 3 dozen cookies

This recipe was given to me by Don's mother, Elizabeth Neely, many years ago. It became a family favorite and can always be found on our Christmas cookie tray.

DEL SHULT NEELY

½ cup (1 stick) margarine

2 beaten eggs

¾ cup sugar

Pinch of salt

1 cup chopped dates

1 cup chopped pecans

1 teaspoon vanilla extract

2 cups Rice Krispies

3 cups sweetened shredded coconut
   (about 7 ounces)

Melt the margarine in a skillet over medium heat. In a bowl, combine the eggs and sugar and add to the butter. Add the salt and chopped dates and cook until thickened, 10 to 15 minutes. Using a wooden spoon, stir the mixture as it cooks and mash the dates to break them down. When thickened, remove from the heat, stir in the nuts, vanilla, and Rice Krispies. Return to the heat and cook for just a few more minutes to help combine the ingredients. Remove from the heat. Using a teaspoon, form into walnut-size balls and roll in shredded coconut.

Peanut Ice Cream Pie

Makes one 9-inch pie

This is a favorite of my children, Callie and Max, when we celebrate Christmas dinner at our house. The recipe can be made bigger by increasing the pie crust size and all other ingredients. Since Max has diabetes, I always use sugar-free ice cream and exclude the peanuts. It is enjoyed by all.

CINDY CALHOUN MILLER

1 (9-inch) graham cracker crust

1 quart vanilla or chocolate ice cream,
   softened

½ cup light corn syrup

⅓ cup creamy peanut butter

⅔ cup chopped, dry roasted unsalted
   peanuts

Press half of the ice cream into the pie crust.

In a small bowl, combine the corn syrup and peanut butter and stir until well blended.

Pour half of the mixture over the ice cream; then sprinkle with half of the peanuts. Repeat, layering with the remainder of the ice cream, the peanut butter mixture, and the peanuts. Freeze until firm, about 3 hours.

Persimmon Cookies

Makes 5 dozen cookies

Look for persimmons in your grocery stores around November. Two persimmons usually equals one cup of pulp. If they are not ripe or soft enough, let them ripen on the kitchen counter. When they are fully ripe, peel off the skin and purée in the blender. Do not include the seeds. I then pour the pulp into a plastic freezer bag (one cup per bag) and store in the freezer until ready for use. This is one of my favorite cookies to bake during the holidays. I never double the recipe. It just does not come out the same. On the day of baking, pull out the frozen pulp to thaw.

CINDY CALHOUN MILLER

½ cup vegetable shortening (Crisco), plus
    more for oiling the cookie sheets

1½ cups sugar

1 egg

1 teaspoon vanilla extract

1 cup persimmon pulp

2 cups flour

1 teaspoon baking soda

1 teaspoon ground cinnamon

1 teaspoon grated nutmeg

½ teaspoon ground cloves

¼ to ½ teaspoon salt

1 cup chopped walnuts (optional)

Preheat the oven to 325°F and oil 2 cookie sheets.

In a bowl, cream together the sugar and shortening. Add the egg and vanilla and beat together. Add the persimmon pulp and mix thoroughly. In another bowl, combine the flour, baking soda, cinnamon, nutmeg, cloves, and salt. Add the dry ingredients to the persimmon mixture. Blend together well. Finally, add the nuts if desired.

Drop by teaspoonfuls onto the cookie sheets. Bake for 15 minutes.

The cookies will look like little puff balls. Once they are cool, I store them in plastic freezer bags or air-tight containers in the freezer. I try to lay them flat in the bags. They will stay fresh in the freezer for a long time so I can use them for holiday gift trays. Keep them somewhat out of sight so they will not all be eaten too quickly!

Persimmon or Fig Cookies

Makes about 10 dozen cookies

BOBBIE LIVERMORE BAIRD

1 cup (2 sticks) margarine, plus more for oiling the cookie sheet

2 cups mashed ripe persimmons or figs, about 4 to 8 persimmons or about 10 figs,
   depending on size

2 teaspoons baking soda

2 cups sugar

2 eggs

4 cups sifted all-purpose flour

1 teaspoon ground cinnamon

½ teaspoon ground cloves

½ teaspoon grated nutmeg

½ teaspoon salt

2 cups chopped walnuts

1 cup raisins or chopped dates

Preheat the oven to 350°F and butter a cookie sheet.

Put the mashed persimmons or figs in a blender, add the baking soda, and purée thoroughly. Set aside for 5 minutes.

In another bowl, cream together the margarine, sugar, and eggs. Add the persimmons or figs to the sugar-egg mixture and blend well. Add the flour, cinnamon, cloves, nutmeg, and salt and mix thoroughly. Drop heaping teaspoonfuls of dough onto the cookie sheet and bake for 15 to 20 minutes.

Bobbie and Doug Baird at
the Livermore family ranch
on Mines Road

Wendy Howe making sure
the recipe is good!

The cookie press with the
ridged disk

 Spritz Cookies

Makes 5 dozen cookies

Granny carried on the Danish tradition of celebrating Christmas on Christmas Eve by inviting friends and relatives for lunch. She served traditional foods such as her famous Danish pickles, open-face sandwiches, and spritzkage or butter cookies. This is her recipe. She used a cookie press, which is needed for these cookies. In the evening, the Holm children, grandchildren, and great-grandchildren opened presents and sang discordant carols. Ione's granddaughters have carried on her tradition of making spritz cookies at Christmastime. In true Holm fashion, they make a party out of it.

IONE TEETER HOLM

2½ cups all-purpose flour
½ teaspoon baking powder
1 cup (2 sticks) butter
¾ cup sugar
Dash salt
1 egg
1 teaspoon vanilla or almond extract

Preheat the oven to 375°F.

Sift together the flour and baking powder. In a bowl, cream together the butter, sugar, and salt. Beat in the egg and vanilla until well mixed. Add the dry ingredients, a little at a time. Put the dough in a cookie press using the ⅛-inch ridged cookie design disk and press the dough out onto cool, unbuttered cookie sheets. Bake until set but not brown, 10 to 12 minutes. Remove from the oven and cut the strips into 3-inch lengths while they are still hot.

We thank our loved ones who have served our country.

Left to right, top to bottom:

Donald J. Diltz, Navy

Gary Holm, Navy Lt. Cdr.

Otto A. Fachner, Army

Leslie Holm (with mother Ida Holm) Army, WWI, served in France

Frank Holm, Air Force, Korean War, stationed on Greenland

Randy Regnolds, Marines, Viet Nam, died in battle in 1969

Bob Gallagher, Navy, and Les Holm Jr., Marines

Ed Teeter (left), Army, WWII, New Zealand and Australia

Daniel A. Fachner, Air Force, served in Germany

James Regnolds, Army, WWII, wounded in Europe

Derek Holm, Air Force

Richie Holm (left), Army, Germany

Wayne Calhoun, Navy, Philippines, 1945

Daniel E. Fachner, Air Force, Arabia, Germany

Not pictured: Robert Holm, Marines, Okinawa, died in battle in 1945; Carl Stebbins, Coast Guard

Granny's Strawberry Ice Cream

Makes 5 quarts

LORI NEELY SOUTH

6 pints ripe strawberries, cleaned and hulled
2 pints heavy whipping cream
1 pint half-and-half
¾ cup sugar
1½ teaspoons vanilla

In a food processor or blender, process 5 pints of the berries until smooth. In a large bowl, combine the fruit with the cream, sugar and vanilla and mix well. Mash the remaining pint of strawberries with a potato masher and stir into the cream mixture.

Freeze in an ice cream maker according to the manufacturer's directions.

Granny's Peach Ice Cream

Makes 4 quarts

LORI NEELY SOUTH

8 ripe medium-size peaches
2 pints heavy whipping cream
1 pint half-and-half
¾ cup sugar
4 tablespoons amaretto

Drop the peaches into a large pot of boiling water and blanch for 2 minutes. Remove them from the water with a slotted spoon and cool. Slip the skins off of the peaches, cut in half, and remove the pits. Process 6 of the peaches in a food processor or blender until smooth. In a large bowl, combine the fruit with the cream, half-and-half, sugar, and amaretto and mix well. Cut the remaining 2 peaches into ¼-inch dice; stir them into the cream mixture.

Freeze in an ice cream maker according to the manufacturer's directions.

Granny saved ice cream making for special summer occasions—such as birthdays, Father's Day, or the Fourth of July. Before she got an electric ice cream maker, the cousins would all get to take turns turning the crank on the old ice cream machine. I can remember all the cousins fighting over who would get to lick the dasher from inside the ice cream machine. Here are my favorites from Granny's ice cream recipes.

—*Lori South*

Granny dishes up her homemade ice cream

Great-grandma Ione, Jamie South, and baby sister Jessica, 1983

Jamie South and son, Brandon Ceballos, 2005

Robert Redford Dessert

Serves 10 to 12

A friend gave me this family recipe when I was in the sixth grade. The idea is that the dessert is so good you drool over it—just as women did over Robert Redford. You can use Heath toffee candy bars instead of the Skor bars. I usually refrigerate this dessert before serving, but you can serve it immediately if you can't wait. For a really chocolaty flavor, use a fudge chocolate cake mix.

JAMIE SOUTH

3 (1.4-ounce) Skor or toffee candy bars
1 (18.25-ounce) chocolate cake mix (makes a 9- by 13-inch cake), prepared per package instructions, cooled
2 (3.4-ounce) packages Jell-o chocolate pudding, prepared per package instructions, cooled
2 (8-ounce) containers Cool Whip, thawed (regular or chocolate flavor)

Place the candy bars in a small paper bag or baggie. Using a rolling pin, pound them until they are broken into small bits. Cut the cooled cake into 3- by 3-inch squares.

Place a few cake squares in the bottom of a medium-size bowl or glass trifle bowl. Cover with a layer of chocolate pudding, then with a layer of Cool Whip. Sprinkle with the candy bits. Continue to layer the cake, pudding, Cool Whip, and candy bits until you reach the top of the bowl, making 2 or 3 layers. Chill for a couple of hours before serving.

Liz's Peach Cobbler

Serves 8

Liz and Matt Thome owned peach orchards in Marysville, California. Ken and Vivian Calhoun's children—Kenny, Jeff, Cindy, and Becky—all worked in the orchards at one time or another. The Thome and Calhoun families spent many summers together camping and fly fishing in Montana, just outside of Yellowstone National Park. The Calhouns loved Montana so much that we built a cabin at Hebgen Lake, where we vacation every year. Liz was a wonderful cook and this recipe brings back so many special memories.

KENNY CALHOUN

Topping
1 cup sugar
½ cup (1 stick) butter or margarine
1 egg
1 teaspoon vanilla extract
1 cup all-purpose flour
2 teaspoons baking powder
½ teaspoon salt
⅓ cup milk

Fruit filling
4 to 6 peaches, peeled and sliced
¼ cup sugar
¼ cup boiling water

Preheat the oven to 350°F.

In a mixing bowl, cream together the sugar and butter. Mix together the egg, vanilla, flour, baking powder, and salt. Add the milk and mix well. The dough will be softer than biscuit dough.

Place the peaches in a deep 11- by 7-inch casserole dish and sprinkle with the sugar. Pour the boiling water over the fruit. Cover the peaches with spoonfuls of dough.

Bake for 15 minutes. Reduce the heat to 325°F and bake for approximately 1 hour or until the topping is golden brown.

Espresso Granita

Serves 4

We made this for our Italian gourmet dinner. We served it after the soup and salad. It was wonderful! The preparation time is about three hours, but it is well worth it. I use my ice shaver to shave the granita. You can also scrape it by hand. If you use an ice shaver, freeze the espresso in the tubs that come with the ice shaver.

BECKY CALHOUN FOSTER

1 cup freshly brewed espresso
¼ cup sugar
1 cup cold water

Pour the hot espresso into a bowl and add the sugar. Stir briskly until the sugar dissolves. Stir in the cold water. Cool to room temperature.

Pour the mixture into a 9- by 13- by 2-inch pan. Place in the freezer for 30 minutes. Stir the frozen crystals from the edges of the pan back into the liquid. As the mixture freezes, scrape a spoon against the sides and the bottom of the pan to loosen and break up any frozen crystals. Repeat the scraping process every 30 minutes until the mixture is frozen and a bit creamy, about 3 hours. Scoop into individual bowls or goblets and serve immediately.

Merritt Hospital student nurses put on a follies. Gladys Holm is at the far right.

Flødeboller (Cream Puffs)

IDA JESSEN HOLM

¼ cup (½ stick) butter or margarine, plus
    more for oiling the cookie sheets
½ cup boiling water
½ cup sifted all-purpose flour
¼ teaspoon salt
2 eggs
½ pint heavy whipping cream
¼ teaspoon vanilla extract
1 tablespoon sugar

Preheat the oven to 450°F. Lightly butter the cookie sheets.

In a medium saucepan over high heat, melt the butter in the boiling water. Decrease the heat to low. Add the flour and salt all at once, stirring vigorously with a spoon until the mixture leaves the sides of the pan in a smooth, compact mass and a metal spoon pressed into it leaves a clear impression.

Immediately remove from the heat. Quickly beat in the eggs, 1 at a time, beating until each is blended and the mixture is smooth. Continue beating the mixture with a spoon until it forms a stiff dough.

Drop by heaping tablespoonfuls (it helps to use a wet spoon) 2 inches apart on a cookie sheet. Using a wet spoon, shape into rounds that point up in the center, like a Hershey's Kiss. Bake for 10 minutes, then decrease the temperature to 400°F and continue baking for another 25 minutes. The cream puffs should be puffed high and golden brown. Remove from the cookie sheets with a spatula and place on a wire cake rack to cool.

Combine the cream, vanilla, and sugar in a bowl. Whip until soft peaks form.

To serve, split the cream puffs almost all the way around horizontally. Fill with a large scoop of fresh whipped cream.

Ida and Carl Holm
fiftieth wedding anniversary

Index

THIS CERTIFIES THAT

The RITE of

Holy Matrimony

WAS CELEBRATED BETWEEN

Daniel M Teeter of Pleasanton Almeda co Cal

and Caroline E Renett of Sunol app Alec Jane co

on the 27 Day off June at Alexandre Almeda co Cal

in the year off our lord 1870

by Geo White Justice off the Peace

Witness   Witness

Holy Bible

F. Bourquin Lith Phila